Bret Harte

Susy

A story of the plains

Bret Harte

Susy
A story of the plains

ISBN/EAN: 9783743303140

Manufactured in Europe, USA, Canada, Australia, Japa

Cover: Foto ©ninafisch / pixelio.de

Manufactured and distributed by brebook publishing software
(www.brebook.com)

Bret Harte

Susy

By the same Author.

POEMS. *Cabinet Edition.* 16mo, $1.00.
Household Edition. 12mo, $1.50; full gilt, $2.00.
EAST AND WEST POEMS. 16mo, $1.50.
THE LUCK OF ROARING CAMP, etc. 16mo, $1.25.
THE LUCK OF ROARING CAMP, and other Stories. In Riverside Aldine Series. 16mo, $1.00.
MRS. SKAGGS'S HUSBANDS, etc. 16mo, $1.25.
TALES OF THE ARGONAUTS. 16mo, $1.25.
THANKFUL BLOSSOM. 18mo, $1.00.
TWO MEN OF SANDY BAR. A Play. 18mo, $1.00.
THE STORY OF A MINE. 18mo, $1.00.
DRIFT FROM TWO SHORES. 18mo, $1.00.
THE TWINS OF TABLE MOUNTAIN, etc. 18mo, $1.00.
WORKS. 6 vols. crown 8vo, each $2.00.
FLIP, and Found at Blazing Star. 18mo, $1.00.
IN THE CARQUINEZ WOODS. 18mo, $1.00.
ON THE FRONTIER. 18mo, $1.00.
BY SHORE AND SEDGE. 18mo, $1.00.
MARUJA. 18mo, $1.00.
SNOW-BOUND AT EAGLE'S. 18mo, $1.00.
A MILLIONAIRE OF ROUGH-AND-READY. 18mo, $1.00.
A WAIF OF THE PLAINS. 18mo, $1.00.
A PHYLLIS OF THE SIERRAS, etc. 18mo, $1.00.
THE ARGONAUTS OF NORTH LIBERTY. 18mo, $1.00.
NOVELS AND TALES. 15 vols. 18mo, $15.00.
THE QUEEN OF THE PIRATE ISLE. A Child's Story, illustrated by KATE GREENAWAY. Square 8vo, $1.50.
THE CRUSADE OF THE EXCELSIOR. Illustrated. $1.25.
CRESSY. 16mo, $1.25.
THE HERITAGE OF DEDLOW MARSH, etc. 16mo, $1.25.
A WARD OF THE GOLDEN GATE. $1.25; paper, 50 cents.
A SAPPHO OF GREEN SPRINGS. 16mo, $1.25.
A FIRST FAMILY OF TASAJARA. 16mo, $1.25.
COLONEL STARBOTTLE'S CLIENT. 16mo, $1.25.
SUSY. 16mo, $1.25.

HOUGHTON, MIFFLIN AND COMPANY,
BOSTON AND NEW YORK.

SUSY

A STORY OF THE PLAINS

BY

BRET HARTE

BOSTON AND NEW YORK
HOUGHTON, MIFFLIN AND COMPANY
The Riverside Press, Cambridge
1893

The Riverside Press, Cambridge, Mass., U. S. A.
Electrotyped and Printed by H. O. Houghton & Company.

SUSY.

CHAPTER I.

WHERE the San Leandro turnpike stretches its dusty, hot, and interminable length along the valley, at a point where the heat and dust have become intolerable, the monotonous expanse of wild oats on either side illimitable, and the distant horizon apparently remoter than ever, it suddenly slips between a stunted thicket or hedge of "scrub oaks," which until that moment had been undistinguishable above the long, misty, quivering level of the grain. The thicket rising gradually in height, but with a regular slope whose gradient had been determined by centuries of western trade winds, presently becomes a fair wood of live-oak, and a few hundred yards further at last assumes the aspect of a primeval forest. A delicious coolness fills the air; the long, shadowy aisles greet the aching eye with a

soothing twilight; the murmur of unseen
brooks is heard, and, by a strange irony, the
enormous, widely-spaced stacks of wild oats
are replaced by a carpet of tiny-leaved
mosses and chickweed at the roots of trees,
and the minutest clover in more open spaces.
The baked and cracked adobe soil of the
now vanished plains is exchanged for a
heavy red mineral dust and gravel, rocks
and boulders make their appearance, and at
times the road is crossed by the white veins
of quartz. It is still the San Leandro turnpike, — a few miles later to rise from this
cañada into the upper plains again, — but
it is also the actual gateway and avenue to
the Robles Rancho. When the departing
visitors of Judge Peyton, now owner of the
rancho, reach the outer plains again, after
twenty minutes' drive from the house, the
cañada, rancho, and avenue have as completely disappeared from view as if they had
been swallowed up in the plain.

A cross road from the turnpike is the
usual approach to the *casa* or mansion, — a
long, low quadrangle of brown adobe wall
in a bare but gently sloping eminence. And
here a second surprise meets the stranger.
He seems to have emerged from the forest

upon another illimitable plain, but one
utterly trackless, wild, and desolate. It is,
however, only a lower terrace of the same
valley, and, in fact, comprises the three
square leagues of the Robles Rancho. Un-
cultivated and savage as it appears, given
over to wild cattle and horses that sometimes
sweep in frightened bands around the very
casa itself, the long south wall of the corral
embraces an orchard of gnarled pear-trees,
an old vineyard, and a venerable garden
of olives and oranges. A manor, formerly
granted by Charles V. to Don Vincente
Robles, of Andalusia, of pious and ascetic
memory, it had commended itself to Judge
Peyton, of Kentucky, a modern heretic
pioneer of bookish tastes and secluded habits, who had bought it of Don Vincente's
descendants. Here Judge Peyton seemed
to have realized his idea of a perfect climate, and a retirement, half-studious, half-
active, with something of the seignioralty of
the old slaveholder that he had been. Here,
too, he had seen the hope of restoring his
wife's health — for which he had undertaken the overland emigration — more
than fulfilled in Mrs. Peyton's improved
physical condition, albeit at the expense,

perhaps, of some of the languorous graces of ailing American wifehood.

It was with a curious recognition of this latter fact that Judge Peyton watched his wife crossing the *patio* or courtyard with her arm around the neck of her adopted daughter "Suzette." A sudden memory crossed his mind of the first day that he had seen them together, — the day that he had brought the child and her boy-companion — two estrays from an emigrant train on the plains — to his wife in camp. Certainly Mrs. Peyton was stouter and stronger fibred; the wonderful Californian climate had materialized her figure, as it had their Eastern fruits and flowers, but it was stranger that "Susy" — the child of homelier frontier blood and parentage, whose wholesome peasant plumpness had at first attracted them — should have grown thinner and more graceful, and even seemed to have gained the delicacy his wife had lost. Six years had imperceptibly wrought this change; it had never struck him before so forcibly as on this day of Susy's return from the convent school at Santa Clara for the holidays.

The woman and child had reached the

broad veranda which, on one side of the
patio, replaced the old Spanish corridor.
It was the single modern innovation that
Peyton had allowed himself when he had
broken the quadrangular symmetry of the
old house with a wooden "annexe" or addition beyond the walls. It made a pleasant
lounging-place, shadowed from the hot mid-
day sun by sloping roofs and awnings, and
sheltered from the boisterous afternoon
trade winds by the opposite side of the
court. But Susy did not seem inclined to
linger there long that morning, in spite of
Mrs. Peyton's evident desire for a maternal
tête-à-tête. The nervous preoccupation and
capricious ennui of an indulged child showed
in her pretty but discontented face, and
knit her curved eyebrows, and Peyton saw
a look of pain pass over his wife's face as
the young girl suddenly and half-laughingly
broke away and fluttered off towards the old
garden.

Mrs. Peyton looked up and caught her
husband's eye.

"I am afraid Susy finds it more dull here
every time she returns," she said, with an
apologetic smile. "I am glad she has invited one of her school friends to come for

a visit to-morrow. You know, yourself, John," she added, with a slight partisan attitude, "that the lonely old house and wild plain are not particularly lively for young people, however much they may suit *your* ways."

"It certainly must be dull if she can't stand it for three weeks in the year," said her husband dryly. "But we really cannot open the San Francisco house for her summer vacation, nor can we move from the rancho to a more fashionable locality. Besides, it will do her good to run wild here. I can remember when she was n't so fastidious. In fact, I was thinking just now how changed she was from the day when we picked her up " —

"How often am I to remind you, John," interrupted the lady, with some impatience, "that we agreed never to speak of her past, or even to think of her as anything but our own child. You know how it pains me! And the poor dear herself has forgotten it, and thinks of us only as her own parents. I really believe that if that wretched father and mother of hers had not been killed by the Indians, or were to come to life again, she would neither know them nor care for them. I mean, of course, John," she said, averting her eyes from a slightly cynical smile on her husband's face, "that it's only natural for young children to be forgetful, and ready to take new impressions."

"And as long, dear, as *we* are not the subjects of this youthful forgetfulness, and she is n't really finding *us* as stupid as the rancho," replied her husband cheerfully, " I suppose we must n't complain."

"John, how can you talk such nonsense?" said Mrs. Peyton impatiently. "But I have no fear of that," she added, with a slightly ostentatious confidence. "I only wish I was as sure "—

"Of what?"

"Of nothing happening that could take her from us. I do not mean death, John, —like our first little one. That does not happen to one twice; but I sometimes dread "—

"What? She's only fifteen, and it's rather early to think about the only other inevitable separation, — marriage. Come, Ally, this is mere fancy. She has been given up to us by her family, — at least, by all that we know are left of them. I have legally adopted her. If I have not made

her my heiress, it is because I prefer to
leave everything to *you,* and I would rather
she should know that she was dependent
upon you for the future than upon me."

"And I can make a will in her favor if I
want to?" said Mrs. Peyton quickly.

"Always," responded her husband smilingly; "but you have ample time to think
of that, I trust. Meanwhile I have some
news for you which may make Susy's visit
to the rancho this time less dull to her.
You remember Clarence Brant, the boy
who was with her when we picked her up,
and who really saved her life?"

"No, I don't," said Mrs. Peyton pet-
tishly, "nor do I want to! You know,
John, how distasteful and unpleasant it is
for me to have those dreary, petty, and vulgar details of the poor child's past life recalled, and, thank Heaven, I have forgotten
them except when you choose to drag them
before me. You agreed, long ago, that we
were never to talk of the Indian massacre of
her parents, so that we could also ignore it
before her; then why do you talk of her
vulgar friends, who are just as unpleasant?
Please let us drop the past."

"Willingly, my dear; but, unfortunately,

we cannot make others do it. And this is a case in point. It appears that this boy, whom we brought to Sacramento to deliver to a relative " —

"And who was a wicked little impostor, — you remember that yourself, John, for he said that he was the son of Colonel Brant, and that he was dead; and you know, and my brother Harry knew, that Colonel Brant was alive all the time, and that he was lying, and Colonel Brant was not his father," broke in Mrs. Peyton impatiently.

"As it seems you do remember that much," said Peyton dryly, "it is only just to him that I should tell you that it appears that he was not an impostor. His story was *true*. I have just learned that Colonel Brant *was* actually his father, but had concealed his lawless life here, as well as his identity, from the boy. He was really that vague relative to whom Clarence was confided, and under that disguise he afterwards protected the boy, had him carefully educated at the Jesuit College of San José, and, dying two years ago in that filibuster raid in Mexico, left him a considerable fortune."

"And what has he to do with Susy's holidays?" said Mrs. Peyton, with uneasy quickness. "John, you surely cannot expect her ever to meet this common creature again, with his vulgar ways. His wretched associates like that Jim Hooker, and, as you yourself admit, the blood of an assassin, duelist, and — Heaven knows what kind of a pirate his father was n't at the last — in his veins! You don't believe that a lad of this type, however much of his father's ill-gotten money he may have, can be fit company for your daughter? You never could have thought of inviting him here?"

"I 'm afraid that 's exactly what I have done, Ally," said the smiling but unmoved Peyton; "but I 'm still more afraid that your conception of his present condition is an unfair one, like your remembrance of his past. Father Sobriente, whom I met at San José yesterday, says he is very intelligent, and thoroughly educated, with charming manners and refined tastes. His father's money, which they say was an investment for him in Carson's Bank five years ago, is as good as any one's, and his father's blood won't hurt him in California or the Southwest. At least, he is received everywhere, and Don Juan Robinson was his guardian. Indeed, as far as social status goes, it might be a serious question if the actual daughter of the late John Silsbee, of Pike County, and the adopted child of John Peyton was in the least his superior. As Father Sobriente evidently knew Clarence's former companionship with Susy and her parents, it would be hardly politic for us to ignore it or seem to be ashamed of it. So I intrusted Sobriente with an invitation to young Brant on the spot."

Mrs. Peyton's impatience, indignation, and opposition, which had successively given way before her husband's quiet, masterful good humor, here took the form of a neurotic fatalism. She shook her head with superstitious resignation.

"Did n't I tell you, John, that I always had a dread of something coming" —

"But if it comes in the shape of a shy young lad, I see nothing singularly portentous in it. They have not met since they were quite small; their tastes have changed; if they don't quarrel and fight they may be equally bored with each other. Yet until then, in one way or another, Clarence will occupy the young lady's vacant caprice, and

her school friend, Mary Rogers, will be
here, you know, to divide his attentions,
and," added Peyton, with mock solemnity,
"preserve the interest of strict propriety.
Shall I break it to her, — or will you?"

"No, — yes." hesitated Mrs. Peyton;
"perhaps I had better."

"Very well, I leave his character in your
hands; only don't prejudice her into a romantic fancy for him." And Judge Peyton
lounged smilingly away.

Then two little tears forced themselves
from Mrs. Peyton's eyes. Again she saw
that prospect of uninterrupted companionship with Susy, upon which each successive
year she had built so many maternal hopes
and confidences, fade away before her. She
dreaded the coming of Susy's school friend,
who shared her daughter's present thoughts
and intimacy, although she had herself invited her in a more desperate dread of the
child's abstracted, discontented eyes; she
dreaded the advent of the boy who had
shared Susy's early life before she knew
her; she dreaded the ordeal of breaking the
news and perhaps seeing that pretty animation spring into her eyes, which she had begun to believe no solicitude or tenderness of

her own ever again awakened, — and yet
she dreaded still more that her husband
should see it too. For the love of this re-
created woman, although not entirely materialized with her changed fibre, had nevertheless become a coarser selfishness fostered
by her loneliness and limited experience.
The maternal yearning left unsatisfied by
the loss of her first-born had never been
filled by Susy's thoughtless acceptance of
it; she had been led astray by the child's
easy transference of dependence and the
forgetfulness of youth, and was only now
dimly conscious of finding herself face to
face with an alien nature.

She started to her feet and followed the
direction that Susy had taken. For a moment she had to front the afternoon trade
wind which chilled her as it swept the plain
beyond the gateway, but was stopped by the
adobe wall, above whose shelter the stunted
treetops — through years of exposure —
slanted as if trimmed by gigantic shears.
At first, looking down the venerable alley of
fantastic, knotted shapes, she saw no trace
of Susy. But half way down the gleam of
a white skirt against a thicket of dark olives
showed her the young girl sitting on a bench

in a neglected arbor. In the midst of this
formal and faded pageantry she looked
charmingly fresh, youthful, and pretty; and
yet the unfortunate woman thought that her
attitude and expression at that moment suggested more than her fifteen years of girl-
hood. Her golden hair still hung unfet-
tered over her straight, boy-like back and
shoulders; her short skirt still showed her
childish feet and ankles; yet there seemed
to be some undefined maturity or a vague
womanliness about her that stung Mrs.
Peyton's heart. The child was growing
away from her, too!

"Susy!"

The young girl raised her head quickly;
her deep violet eyes seemed also to leap with
a sudden suspicion, and with a half-mechan-
ical, secretive movement, that might have
been only a schoolgirl's instinct, her right
hand had slipped a paper on which she
was scribbling between the leaves of her
book. Yet the next moment, even while
looking interrogatively at her mother, she
withdrew the paper quietly, tore it up
into small pieces, and threw them on the
ground.

But Mrs. Peyton was too preoccupied

with her news to notice the circumstance, and too nervous in her haste to be tactful. "Susy, your father has invited that boy, Clarence Brant, — you know that creature we picked up and assisted on the plains, when you were a mere baby, — to come down here and make us a visit."

Her heart seemed to stop beating as she gazed breathlessly at the girl. But Susy's face, unchanged except for the alert, questioning eyes, remained fixed for a moment; then a childish smile of wonder opened her small red mouth, expanded it slightly as she said simply: —

"Lor, mar! He has n't, really!"

Inexpressibly, yet unreasonably reassured, Mrs. Peyton hurriedly recounted her husband's story of Clarence's fortune, and was even joyfully surprised into some fairness of statement.

"But you don't remember him much, do you, dear? It was so long ago, and — you are quite a young lady now," she added eagerly.

The open mouth was still fixed; the wondering smile would have been idiotic in any face less dimpled, rosy, and piquant than Susy's. After a slight gasp, as if in still

incredulous and partly reminiscent preoccupation, she said without replying: —

"How funny!   When is he coming?"

"Day after to-morrow," returned Mrs.
Peyton, with a contented smile.

"And Mary Rogers will be here, too.   It
will be real fun for her."

Mrs. Peyton was more than reassured.
Half ashamed of her jealous fears, she drew
Susy's golden head towards her and kissed
it.   And the young girl, still reminiscent,
with smilingly abstracted toleration, returned the caress.

CHAPTER II.

It was not thought inconsistent with Susy's capriciousness that she should declare her intention the next morning of driving her pony buggy to Santa Inez to anticipate the stage-coach and fetch Mary Rogers from the station. Mrs. Peyton, as usual, supported the young lady's whim and opposed her husband's objections.

"Because the stage-coach happens to pass our gate, John, it is no reason why Susy should n't drive her friend from Santa Inez if she prefers it. It 's only seven miles, and you can send Pedro to follow her on horseback to see that she comes to no harm."

"But that is n't Pedro's business," said Peyton.

"He ought to be proud of the privilege," returned the lady, with a toss of her head.

Peyton smiled grimly, but yielded; and when the stage-coach drew up the next afternoon at the Santa Inez Hotel, Susy was already waiting in her pony carriage before

it. Although the susceptible driver, ex-
pressman, and passengers generally, charmed
with this golden-haired vision, would have
gladly protracted the meeting of the two
young friends, the transfer of Mary Rogers
from the coach to the carriage was effected
with considerable hauteur and youthful dignity by Susy. Even Mary Rogers, two
years Susy's senior, a serious brunette,
whose good-humor did not, however, impair
her capacity for sentiment, was impressed
and even embarrassed by her demeanor; but
only for a moment. When they had driven
from the hotel and were fairly hidden again
in the dust of the outlying plain, with the
discreet Pedro hovering in the distance,
Susy dropped the reins, and, grasping her
companion's arm, gasped, in tones of dramatic intensity: —

"He's been heard from, and is coming
here!"

"Who?"

A sickening sense that her old confidante
had already lost touch with her — they had
been separated for nearly two weeks — might
have passed through Susy's mind.

"Who?" she repeated, with a vicious
shake of Mary's arm, "why, Clarence Brant,
of course."

"No!" said Mary, vaguely.

Nevertheless, Susy went on rapidly, as if to neutralize the effect of her comrade's vacuity.

"You never could have imagined it! Never! Even *I*, when mother told me, I thought I should have fainted, and *all* would have been revealed!"

"But," hesitated the still wondering confidante, "I thought that was all over long ago. You have n't seen him nor heard from him since that day you met accidentally at Santa Clara, two years ago, have you?"

Susy's eyes shot a blue ray of dark but unutterable significance into Mary's, and then were carefully averted. Mary Rogers, although perfectly satisfied that Susy had never seen Clarence since, nevertheless instantly accepted and was even thrilled with this artful suggestion of a clandestine correspondence. Such was the simple faith of youthful friendship.

"Mother knows nothing of it, of course, and a word from you or him would ruin everything," continued the breathless Susy. "That 's why I came to fetch you and warn you. You must see him first, and warn him at any cost. If I had n't run every risk to come here to-day, Heaven knows what might have happened! What do you think of the ponies, dear? They 're my own, and the sweetest! This one 's Susy, that one Clarence, — but privately, you know. Before the world and in the stables he 's only Birdie.''

"But I thought you wrote to me that you called them 'Paul and Virginie,'" said Mary doubtfully.

"I do, sometimes," said Susy calmly. "But one has to learn to suppress one's feelings, dear!" Then quickly, "I do so hate deceit, don't you? Tell me, don't you think deceit perfectly hateful?"

Without waiting for her friend's loyal assent, she continued rapidly: "And he 's just rolling in wealth! and educated, papa says, to the highest degree!"

"Then," began Mary, "if he 's coming with your mother's consent, and if you have n't quarreled, and it is not broken off, I should think you 'd be just delighted."

But another quick flash from Susy's eyes dispersed these beatific visions of the future. "Hush!" she said, with suppressed dramatic intensity. "You know not what you say! There 's an awful mystery hangs over him.

Mary Rogers," continued the young girl, approaching her small mouth to her confidante's ear in an appalling whisper. "His father was — a *pirate!* Yes — lived a pirate and was killed a pirate!"

The statement, however, seemed to be partly ineffective. Mary Rogers was startled but not alarmed, and even protested feebly. "But," she said, "if the father's dead, what's that to do with Clarence? He was always with your papa — so you told me, dear — or other people, and could n't catch anything from his own father. And I'm sure, dearest, he always seemed nice and quiet."

"Yes, *seemed*," returned Susy darkly, "but that's all you know! It was in *his blood*. You know it always is, — you read it in the books, — you could see it in his eye. There were times, my dear, when he was thwarted, — when the slightest attention from another person to me revealed it! I have kept it to myself, — but think, dearest, of the effects of jealousy on that passionate nature! Sometimes I tremble to look back upon it."

Nevertheless, she raised her hands and threw back her lovely golden mane from her childish shoulders with an easy, untroubled gesture. It was singular that Mary Rogers, leaning back comfortably in the buggy, also accepted these heart-rending revelations with comfortably knitted brows and luxuriously contented concern. If she found it difficult to recognize in the picture just drawn by Susy the quiet, gentle, and sadly reserved youth she had known, she said nothing. After a silence, lazily watching the distant wheeling vacquero, she said: —

"And your father always sends an outrider like that with you? How nice! So picturesque — and like the old Spanish days."

"Hush!" said Susy, with another unutterable glance.

But this time Mary was in full sympathetic communion with her friend, and equal to any incoherent hiatus of revelation.

"No!" she said promptly, "you don't mean it!"

"Don't ask me. I dare n't say anything to papa, for he 'd be simply furious. But there are times when we 're alone, and Pedro wheels down so near with *such* a look in his black eyes, that I 'm all in a tremble. It 's dreadful! They say he 's a real Briones, — and he sometimes says something in Spanish, ending with 'señorita,' but I pretend I don't understand."

"And I suppose that if anything should happen to the ponies, he'd just risk his life to save you."

"Yes, — and it would be so awful, — for I just hate him!"

"But if *I* was with you, dear, he couldn't expect you to be as grateful as if you were alone. Susy!" she continued after a pause, "if you just stirred up the ponies a little so as to make 'em go fast, perhaps he might think they'd got away from you, and come dashing down here. It would be so funny to see him, — wouldn't it?"

The two girls looked at each other; their eyes sparkled already with a fearful joy, — they drew a long breath of guilty anticipation. For a moment Susy even believed in her imaginary sketch of Pedro's devotion.

"Papa said I wasn't to use the whip except in a case of necessity," she said, reaching for the slender silver-handled toy, and setting her pretty lips together with the added determination of disobedience. "G'long!" — and she laid the lash smartly on the shining backs of the animals.

They were wiry, slender brutes of Mojave
Indian blood, only lately broken to harness,
and still undisciplined in temper. The lash
sent them rearing into the air, where, forget-
ting themselves in the slackened traces and
loose reins, they came down with a succession of bounds that brought the light buggy
leaping after them with its wheels scarcely
touching the ground. That unlucky lash
had knocked away the bonds of a few
months' servitude and sent the half-broken
brutes instinctively careering with arched
backs and kicking heels into the field towards the nearest cover.

Mary Rogers cast a hurried glance over
her shoulder. Alas, they had not calcu-
lated on the insidious levels of the terraced
plain, and the faithful Pedro had suddenly
disappeared; the intervention of six inches
of rising wild oats had wiped him out of the
prospect and their possible salvation as completely as if he had been miles away. Nevertheless, the girls were not frightened;
perhaps they had not time. There was,
however, the briefest interval for the most
dominant of feminine emotions, and it was
taken advantage of by Susy.

"It was all *your* fault, dear!" she gasped,

as the forewheels of the buggy, dropping
into a gopher rut, suddenly tilted up the
back of the vehicle and shot its fair occu-
pants into the yielding palisades of dusty
grain. The shock detached the whiffletree
from the splinter-bar, snapped the light pole,
and, turning the now thoroughly frightened animals again from their course, sent
them, goaded by the clattering fragments,
flying down the turnpike. Half a mile
farther on they overtook the gleaming white
canvas hood of a slowly moving wagon
drawn by two oxen, and, swerving again,
the nearer pony stepped upon a trailing
trace and ingloriously ended their career by
rolling himself and his companion in the
dust at the very feet of the peacefully plodding team.

Equally harmless and inglorious was the
catastrophe of Susy and her friend. The
strong, elastic stalks of the tall grain broke
their fall and enabled them to scramble to
their feet, dusty, disheveled, but unhurt,
and even unstunned by the shock. Their
first instinctive cries over a damaged hat or
ripped skirt were followed by the quick
reaction of childish laughter. They were
alone; the very defection of Pedro consoled

them, in its absence of any witness to their disaster; even their previous slight attitude to each other was forgotten. They groped their way, pushing and panting, to the road again, where, beholding the overset buggy with its wheels ludicrously in the air, they suddenly seized and shook each other, and in an outburst of hilarious ecstasy, fairly laughed until the tears came into their eyes.

Then there was a breathless silence.

"The stage will be coming by in a moment," composedly said Susy. "Fix me, dear."

Mary Rogers calmly walked around her friend, bestowing a practical shake there, a pluck here, completely retying one bow and restoring an engaging fullness to another, yet critically examining, with her head on one side, the fascinating result. Then Susy performed the same function for Mary with equal deliberation and deftness. Suddenly Mary started and looked up.

"It's coming," she said quickly, "and they've *seen us.*"

The expression of the faces of the two girls instantly changed. A pained dignity and resignation, apparently born of the most harrowing experiences and controlled only by perfect good breeding, was distinctly suggested in their features and attitude as they stood patiently by the wreck of their overturned buggy awaiting the oncoming coach. In sharp contrast was the evident excitement among the passengers. A few rose from their seats in their eagerness; as the stage pulled up in the road beside the buggy four or five of the younger men leaped to the ground.

"Are you hurt, miss?" they gasped sympathetically.

Susy did not immediately reply, but ominously knitted her pretty eyebrows as if repressing a spasm of pain. Then she said, "Not at all," coldly, with the suggestion of stoically concealing some lasting or perhaps fatal injury, and took the arm of Mary Rogers, who had, in the mean time, established a touching yet graceful limp.

Declining the proffered assistance of the passengers, they helped each other into the coach, and freezingly requesting the driver to stop at Mr. Peyton's gate, maintained a statuesque and impressive silence. At the gates they got down, followed by the sympathetic glances of the others.

To all appearance their escapade, albeit

fraught with dangerous possibilities, had
happily ended. But in the economy of human affairs, as in nature, forces are not
suddenly let loose without more or less sympathetic disturbance which is apt to linger
after the impelling cause is harmlessly
spent. The fright which the girls had un-
successfully attempted to produce in the
heart of their escort had passed him to become a panic elsewhere. Judge Peyton,
riding near the gateway of his rancho, was
suddenly confronted by the spectacle of one
of his vacqueros driving on before him the
two lassoed and dusty ponies, with a face
that broke into violent gesticulating at his
master's quick interrogation.

"Ah! Mother of God! It was an evil
day! For the bronchos had run away, upset the buggy, and had only been stopped
by a brave *Americano* of an ox-team, whose
lasso was even now around their necks, to
prove it, and who had been dragged a matter of a hundred *varas*, like a calf, at their
heels. The señoritas, — ah! had he not
already said they were safe, by the mercy
of Jesus! — picked up by the coach, and
would be here at this moment."

"But where was Pedro all the time?

What was he doing ? " demanded Peyton,
with a darkened face and gathering anger.

The vacquero looked at his master, and
shrugged his shoulders significantly.   At
any other time Peyton would have remembered that Pedro, as the reputed scion of a
decayed Spanish family, and claiming superiority, was not a favorite with his fellow-
retainers.   But the gesture, half of suggestion, half of depreciation, irritated Peyton
still more.

. "Well, where is this American who *did*
something when there was n't a man among
you all able to˙ stop a child's runaway
ponies?" he said sarcastically.   "Let me
see him."

The vacquero became still more depre-
catory.

"Ah! He had driven on with his team
towards San Antonio. He would not stop
to be thanked.   But that was the whole
truth. He, Incarnacion, could swear to it
as to the Creed. There was nothing more."

"Take those beasts around the back way
to the corral," said Peyton, thoroughly en-
raged, "and not a word of this to any one at
the *casa*, do you hear? Not a word to Mrs.
Peyton or the servants, or, by Heaven, I'll

clear the rancho of the whole lazy crew of
you at once. Out of the way there, and be
off!''

He spurred his horse past the frightened
menial, and dashed down the narrow lane
that led to the gate. But, as Incarnacion
had truly said, "It was an evil day," for at
the bottom of the lane, ambling slowly along
as he lazily puffed a yellow cigarette, appeared the figure of the erring Pedro. Utterly unconscious of the accident, attribut-
ing the disappearance of his charges to the
inequalities of the plain, and, in truth, little
interested in what he firmly believed was his
purely artificial function, he had even made
a larger circuit to stop at a wayside *fonda*
for refreshments.

Unfortunately, there is no more illogical
sequence of human emotion than the exas-
peration produced by the bland manner of
the unfortunate object who has excited it,
although that very unconcern may be the
convincing proof of innocence of intention.
Judge Peyton, already influenced, was furious at the comfortable obliviousness of his
careless henchman, and rode angrily towards
him. Only a quick turn of Pedro's wrist
kept the two men from coming into colli-
sion.

"Is this the way you attend to your duty?" demanded Peyton, in a thick, suppressed voice. "Where is the buggy? Where is my daughter?"

There was no mistaking Judge Peyton's manner, even if the reason of it was not so clear to Pedro's mind, and his hot Latin blood flew instinctively to his face. But for that, he might have shown some concern or asked an explanation. As it was, he at once retorted with the national shrug and the national half-scornful, half-lazy " *Quien sabe?* "

"Who knows?" repeated Peyton, hotly. " *I* do! She was thrown out of her buggy through your negligence and infernal laziness! The ponies ran away, and were stopped by a stranger who was n't afraid of risking his bones, while *you* were limping around somewhere like a slouching, cowardly coyote."

The vacquero struggled a moment between blank astonishment and inarticulate rage. At last he burst out: —

"I am no coyote! I was there! I saw no runaway!"

"Don't lie to me, sir!" roared Peyton. "I tell you the buggy was smashed, the girls

were thrown out and nearly killed " — He
stopped suddenly. The sound of youthful
laughter had come from the bottom of the
lane, where Susy Peyton and Mary Rogers,
just alighted from the coach, in the reaction
of their previous constrained attitude, were
flying hilariously into view. A slight embarrassment crossed Peyton's face; a still
deeper flush of anger overspread Pedro's
sullen cheek.

Then Pedro found tongue again, his native one, rapidly, violently, half incoherently. "Ah, yes! It had come to this. It
seems he was not a vacquero, a companion
of the padrone on lands that had been his
own before the *Americanos* robbed him of
it, but a servant, a lackey of *muchachas*, an
attendant on children to amuse them, or —
why not? — an appendage to his daughter's
state! Ah, Jesus Maria! such a state!
such a *muchacha!* A picked-up foundling
— a swineherd's daughter — to be ennobled
by his, Pedro's, attendance, and for whose
vulgar, clownish tricks, — tricks of a swineherd's daughter, — he, Pedro, was to be
brought to book and insulted as if she were
of Hidalgo blood! Ah, Caramba! Don
Juan Peyton would find he could no more

make a servant of him than he could make a lady of her!"

The two young girls were rapidly approaching. Judge Peyton spurred his horse beside the vacquero's, and, swinging the long thong of his bridle ominously in his clenched fingers, said, with a white face:—

" *Vamos!* "

Pedro's hand slid towards his sash. Peyton only looked at him with a rigid smile of scorn.

"Or I 'll lash you here before them both," he added in a lower voice.

The vacquero met Peyton's relentless eyes with a yellow flash of hate, drew his reins sharply, until his mustang, galled by the cruel bit, reared suddenly as if to strike at the immovable American, then, apparently with the same action, he swung it around on its hind legs, as on a pivot, and dashed towards the corral at a furious gallop.

CHAPTER III.

MEANTIME the heroic proprietor of the
peaceful ox-team, whose valor Incarnacion
had so infelicitously celebrated, was walking
listlessly in the dust beside his wagon. At
a first glance his slouching figure, taken in
connection with his bucolic conveyance, did
not immediately suggest a hero. As he
emerged from the dusty cloud it could be
seen that he was wearing a belt from which
a large dragoon revolver and hunting knife
were slung, and placed somewhat ostentatiously across the wagon seat was a rifle.
Yet the other contents of the wagon were of
a singularly inoffensive character, and even
suggested articles of homely barter. Culinary utensils of all sizes, tubs, scullery
brushes, and clocks, with several rolls of
cheap carpeting and calico, might have
been the wares of some traveling vender.
Yet, as they were only visible through a flap
of the drawn curtains of the canvas hood,
they did not mitigate the general aggressive

effect of their owner's appearance. A red bandanna handkerchief knotted and thrown loosely over his shoulders, a slouched hat pulled darkly over a head of long tangled hair, which, however, shadowed a round, comfortable face, scantily and youthfully bearded, were part of these confusing inconsistencies.

The shadows of the team wagon were already lengthening grotesquely over the flat, cultivated fields, which for some time had taken the place of the plains of wild oats in the branch road into which they had turned. The gigantic shadow of the proprietor, occasionally projected before it, was in characteristic exaggeration, and was often obliterated by a puff of dust, stirred by the plodding hoofs of the peaceful oxen, and swept across the field by the strong afternoon trades. The sun sank lower, although a still potent presence above the horizon line; the creaking wagon lumbered still heavily along. Yet at intervals its belligerent proprietor would start up from his slouching, silent march, break out into violent, disproportionate, but utterly ineffective objurgation of his cattle, jump into the air and kick his heels together in some par-

oxysm of indignation against them, — an
act, however, which was received always with
heavy bovine indifference, the dogged scorn
of swaying, repudiating heads, or the dull
contempt of lazily flicking tails.

Towards sunset one or two straggling
barns and cottages indicated their approach
to the outskirts of a country town or settlement. Here the team halted, as if the
belligerent-looking teamster had felt his appearance was inconsistent with an effeminate
civilization, and the oxen were turned into
an open waste opposite a nondescript wooden
tenement, half farmhouse and half cabin,
evidently of the rudest Western origin. He
may have recognized the fact that these
"shanties" were not, as the ordinary traveler might infer, the first rude shelter of the
original pioneers or settlers, but the later
makeshifts of some recent Western immi-
grants who, like himself, probably found
themselves unequal to the settled habits of
the village, and who still retained their
nomadic instincts. It chanced, however,
that the cabin at present was occupied by a
New England mechanic and his family, who
had emigrated by ship around Cape Horn,
and who had no experience of the West,

the plains, or its people. It was therefore
with some curiosity and a certain amount of
fascinated awe that the mechanic's only
daughter regarded from the open door of
her dwelling the arrival of this wild and
lawless-looking stranger.

Meantime he had opened the curtains of
the wagon and taken from its interior a
number of pots, pans, and culinary utensils,
which he proceeded to hang upon certain
hooks that were placed on the outer ribs of
the board and the sides of the vehicle. To
this he added a roll of rag carpet, the end
of which hung from the tailboard, and a roll
of pink calico temptingly displayed on the
seat. The mystification and curiosity of the
young girl grew more intense at these pro-
ceedings. It looked like the ordinary exhibition of a traveling peddler, but the gloomy
and embattled appearance of the man himself scouted so peaceful and commonplace a
suggestion. Under the pretense of chasing
away a marauding hen, she sallied out upon
the waste near the wagon. It then became
evident that the traveler had seen her, and
was not averse to her interest in his movements, although he had not changed his attitude of savage retrospection. An occasional

ejaculation of suppressed passion, as if the
memory of some past conflict was too much
for him, escaped him even in this peaceful
occupation.   As this possibly caused the
young girl to still hover timidly in the distance, he suddenly entered the wagon and
reappeared carrying a tin bucket, with which
he somewhat ostentatiously crossed her path,
his eyes darkly wandering as if seeking
something.

"If you 're lookin' for the spring, it 's a
spell furder on — by the willows."

It was a pleasant voice, the teamster
thought, albeit with a dry, crisp, New England accent unfamiliar to his ears.   He
looked into the depths of an unlovely blue-
check sunbonnet, and saw certain small,
irregular features and a sallow cheek, lit up
by a pair of perfectly innocent, trustful, and
wondering brown eyes.   Their timid possessor seemed to be a girl of seventeen,
whose figure, although apparently clad in
one of her mother's gowns, was still unde-
veloped and repressed by rustic hardship
and innutrition.   As her eyes met his she
saw that the face of this gloomy stranger
was still youthful, by no means implacable,
and, even at that moment, was actually suf-

fused by a brick-colored blush! In matters
of mere intuition, the sex, even in its most
rustic phase, is still our superior; and this
unsophisticated girl, as the trespasser stammered, "Thank ye, miss," was instinctively
emboldened to greater freedom.

"Dad ain't tu hum, but ye kin have a
drink o' milk if ye keer for it."

She motioned shyly towards the cabin, and
then led the way. The stranger, with an
inarticulate murmur, afterwards disguised
as a cough, followed her meekly. Nevertheless, by the time they had reached the
cabin he had shaken his long hair over his
eyes again, and a dark abstraction gathered
chiefly in his eyebrows. But it did not
efface from the girl's mind the previous con-
cession of a blush, and, although it added to
her curiosity, did not alarm her. He drank
the milk awkwardly. But by the laws of
courtesy, even among the most savage tribes,
she felt he was, at that moment at least,
harmless. A timid smile fluttered around
her mouth as she said: —

"When ye hung up them things I thought
ye might be havin' suthing to swap or sell.
That is," — with tactful politeness, — "mother was wantin' a new skillet, and it would

have been handy if you 'd had one. But "
— with an apologetic glance at his equip-
ments — "if it ain't your business, it 's all
right, and no offense."

"I 've got a lot o' skillets," said the
strange teamster, with marked condescen-
sion, "and she can have one. They 're all
that 's left outer a heap o' trader's stuff captured by Injuns t' other side of Laramie.
We had a big fight to get 'em back. Lost
two of our best men, — scalped at Bloody
Creek, — and had to drop a dozen redskins
in their tracks, — me and another man, —
lyin' flat in er wagon and firin' under the
flaps o' the canvas. I don't know ez they
waz wuth it," he added in gloomy retrospect; "but I 've got to get rid of 'em, I
reckon, somehow, afore I work over to Dead-
man's Gulch again."

The young girl's eyes brightened timidly
with a feminine mingling of imaginative awe
and personal, pitying interest. He was,
after all, so young and amiable looking for
such hardships and adventures. And with
all this, he — this Indian fighter — was a
little afraid of *her!*

"Then that 's why you carry that knife
and six - shooter? " she said. "But you

won't want 'em now, here in the settlement."

"That's ez mebbe," said the stranger
darkly. He paused, and then suddenly, as
if recklessly accepting a dangerous risk, un-
buckled his revolver and handed it abstractedly to the young girl. But the sheath of
the bowie-knife was a fixture in his body-
belt, and he was obliged to withdraw the
glittering blade by itself, and to hand it to
her in all its naked terrors. The young girl
received the weapons with a smiling complacency. Upon such altars as these the
skeptical reader will remember that Mars
had once hung his "battered shield," his
lance, and "uncontrolled crest."

Nevertheless, the warlike teamster was
not without embarrassment. Muttering
something about the necessity of "looking
after his stock," he achieved a hesitating
bow, backed awkwardly out of the door, and
receiving from the conquering hands of the
young girl his weapons again, was obliged
to carry them somewhat ingloriously in his
hands across the road, and put them on the
wagon seat, where, in company with the
culinary articles, they seemed to lose their
distinctively aggressive character. Here,

although his cheek was still flushed from his peaceful encounter, his voice regained some of its hoarse severity as he drove the oxen from the muddy pool into which they had luxuriantly wandered, and brought their fodder from the wagon. Later, as the sun was setting, he lit a corn-cob pipe, and somewhat ostentatiously strolled down the road, with a furtive eye lingering upon the still open door of the farmhouse. Presently two angular figures appeared from it, the farmer and his wife, intent on barter.

These he received with his previous gloomy preoccupation, and a slight variation of the story he had told their daughter. It is possible that his suggestive indifference piqued and heightened the bargaining instincts of the woman, for she not only bought the skillet, but purchased a clock and a roll of carpeting. Still more, in some effusion of rustic courtesy, she extended an invitation to him to sup with them, which he declined and accepted in the same embarrassed breath, returning the proffered hospitality by confidentially showing them a couple of dried scalps, presumably of Indian origin. It was in the same moment of human weakness that he answered their po-

lite query as to "what they might call him,"
by intimating that his name was "Red
Jim," — a title of achievement by which he
was generally known, which for the present
must suffice them. But during the repast
that followed this was shortened to "Mister
Jim," and even familiarly by the elders to
plain "Jim." Only the young girl habitually used the formal prefix in return for the
"Miss Phœbe" that he called her.

With three such sympathetic and unex-
perienced auditors the gloomy embarrassment of Red Jim was soon dissipated, although it could hardly be said that he was
generally communicative. Dark tales of
Indian warfare, of night attacks and wild
stampedes, in which he had always taken a
prominent part, flowed freely from his lips,
but little else of his past history or present
prospects. And even his narratives of adventure were more or less fragmentary and
imperfect in detail.

"You woz saying," said the farmer, with
slow, matter of fact, New England deliberation, "ez how you guessed you woz beguiled
amongst the Injins by your Mexican part-
ner, a pow'ful influential man, and yet you
woz the only one escaped the gen'ral slar-

terin'. How came the Injins to kill *him*, —
their friend?"

"They did n't," returned Jim, with ominously averted eyes.

"What became of him?" continued the
farmer.

Red Jim shadowed his eyes with his
hand, and cast a dark glance of scrutiny
out of the doors and windows. The young
girl perceived it with timid, fascinated concern, and said hurriedly: —

"Don't ask him, father! Don't you see
he must n't tell?"

"Not when spies may be hangin' round,
and doggin' me at every step," said Red
Jim, as if reflecting, with another furtive
glance towards the already fading prospect
without. "They 've sworn to revenge him,"
he added moodily.

A momentary silence followed. The
farmer coughed slightly, and looked dubi-
ously at his wife. But the two women had
already exchanged feminine glances of sympathy for this evident slayer of traitors, and
were apparently inclined to stop any ad-
verse criticism.

In the midst of which a shout was heard
from the road. The farmer and his family

instinctively started. Red Jim alone remained unmoved, — a fact which did not les-
sen the admiration of his feminine audience.
The host rose quickly, and went out. The
figure of a horseman had halted in the road,
but after a few moments' conversation with
the farmer they both moved towards the
house and disappeared. When the farmer
returned, it was to say that "one of them
'Frisco dandies, who did n't keer about stop-
pin' at the hotel in the settlement," had
halted to give his "critter" a feed and
drink that he might continue his journey.
He had asked him to come in while the
horse was feeding, but the stranger had
"guessed he'd stretch his legs outside and
smoke his cigar;" he might have thought
the company "not fine enough for him,"
but he was "civil spoken enough, and had
an all-fired smart hoss, and seemed to know
how to run him." To the anxious inqui-
ries of his wife and daughter he added that
the stranger did n't seem like a spy or a
Mexican; was "as young as *him*," pointing
to the moody Red Jim, "and a darned sight
more peaceful-like in style."

Perhaps owing to the criticism of the
farmer, perhaps from some still lurking sus-

picion of being overheard by eavesdroppers,
or possibly from a humane desire to relieve
the strained apprehension of the women,
Red Jim, as the farmer disappeared to rejoin
the stranger, again dropped into a lighter
and gentler vein of reminiscence. He told
them how, when a mere boy, he had been
lost from an emigrant train in company
with a little girl some years his junior.
How, when they found themselves alone on
the desolate plain, with the vanished train
beyond their reach, he endeavored to keep
the child from a knowledge of the real danger of their position, and to soothe and
comfort her. How he carried her on his
back, until, exhausted, he sank in a heap of
sage-brush. How he was surrounded by Indians, who, however, never suspected his
hiding-place; and how he remained motionless and breathless with the sleeping child
for three hours, until they departed. How,
at the last moment, he had perceived a train
in the distance, and had staggered with her
thither, although shot at and wounded by
the trainmen in the belief that he was an
Indian. How it was afterwards discovered
that the child was the long-lost daughter of
a millionaire; how he had resolutely refused

any gratuity for saving her, and she was now a peerless young heiress, famous in California. Whether this lighter tone of narrative suited him better, or whether the active feminine sympathy of his auditors helped him along, certain it was that his story was more coherent and intelligible and his voice less hoarse and constrained than in his previous belligerent reminiscences; his expression changed, and even his features worked into something like gentler emotion. The bright eyes of Phœbe, fastened upon him, turned dim with a faint moisture, and her pale cheek took upon itself a little color. The mother, after interjecting "Du tell," and " I wanter know," remained open-mouthed, staring at her visitor. And in the silence that followed, a pleasant, but somewhat melancholy voice came from the open door.

"I beg your pardon, but I thought I could n't be mistaken. It *is* my old friend, Jim Hooker!"

Everybody started. Red Jim stumbled to his feet with an inarticulate and hysteric exclamation. Yet the apparition that now stood in the doorway was far from being terrifying or discomposing. It was evidently

the stranger, — a slender, elegantly-knit figure, whose upper lip was faintly shadowed
by a soft, dark mustache indicating early
manhood, and whose unstudied ease in his
well-fitting garments bespoke the dweller of
cities. Good-looking and well-dressed, without the consciousness of being either; self-
possessed through easy circumstances, yet
without self-assertion; courteous by nature
and instinct as well as from an experience
of granting favors, he might have been a
welcome addition to even a more critical
company. But Red Jim, hurriedly seizing
his outstretched hand, instantly dragged him
away from the doorway into the road and
out of hearing of his audience.

"Did you hear what I was saying?" he
asked hoarsely.

"Well, yes, — I think so," returned the
stranger, with a quiet smile.

"Ye ain't goin' back on me, Clarence,
are ye, — ain't goin' to gimme away afore
them, old pard, are ye?" said Jim, with a
sudden change to almost pathetic pleading.

"No," returned the stranger, smiling.
"And certainly not before that interested
young lady, Jim. But stop. Let me look
at you."

He held out both hands, took Jim's, spread them apart for a moment with a boyish gesture, and, looking in his face, said half mischievously, half sadly, "Yes, it's the same old Jim Hooker, — unchanged."

"But *you're* changed, — reg'lar war paint, Big Injin style!" said Hooker, looking up at him with an awkward mingling of admiration and envy. "Heard you struck it rich with the old man, and was Mister Brant now!"

"Yes," said Clarence gently, yet with a smile that had not only a tinge of weariness but even of sadness in it.

Unfortunately, the act, which was quite natural to Clarence's sensitiveness, and indeed partly sprang from some concern in his old companion's fortunes, translated itself by a very human process to Hooker's consciousness as a piece of rank affectation. *He* would have been exalted and exultant in Clarence's place, consequently any other exhibition was only "airs." Nevertheless, at the present moment Clarence was to be placated.

"You didn't mind my telling that story about your savin' Susy as my own, did ye?" he said, with a hasty glance over his shoul-

der. "I only did it to fool the old man and
women-folks, and make talk. You won't
blow on me? Ye ain't mad about it?"

It had crossed Clarence's memory that
when they were both younger Jim Hooker
had once not only borrowed his story, but
his name and personality as well. Yet in
his loyalty to old memories there was mingled no resentment for past injury. "Of
course not," he said, with a smile that was,
however, still thoughtful. "Why should I?
Only I ought to tell you that Susy Peyton
is living with her adopted parents not ten
miles from here, and it might reach their
ears. She's quite a young lady now, and
if *I* wouldn't tell her story to strangers, I
don't think *you* ought to, Jim."

He said this so pleasantly that even the
skeptical Jim forgot what he believed were
the "airs and graces" of self-abnegation, and
said, "Let's go inside, and I'll introduce
you," and turned to the house. But Clarence Brant drew back. "I'm going on as
soon as my horse is fed, for I'm on a visit
to Peyton, and I intend to push as far as
Santa Inez still to-night. I want to talk
with you about yourself, Jim," he added
gently; "your prospects and your future.

I heard," he went on hesitatingly, "that you were — at work — in a restaurant in San Francisco. I'm glad to see that you are at least your own master here," — he glanced at the wagon. "You are selling things, I suppose? For yourself, or another? Is that team yours? Come," he added, still pleasantly, but in an older and graver voice, with perhaps the least touch of experienced authority, "be frank, Jim. Which is it? Never mind what things you've told *in there*, tell *me* the truth about yourself. Can I help you in any way? Believe me, I should like to. We have been old friends, whatever difference in our luck, I am yours still."

Thus adjured, the redoubtable Jim, in a hoarse whisper, with a furtive eye on the house, admitted that he was traveling for an itinerant peddler, whom he expected to join later in the settlement; that he had his own methods of disposing of his wares, and (darkly) that his proprietor and the world generally had better not interfere with him; that (with a return to more confidential lightness) he had already "worked the Wild West Injin" business so successfully as to dispose of his wares, particularly in yonder house, and might do even more if not prematurely and wantonly "blown upon," "gone back on," or "given away."

"But would n't you like to settle down on some bit of land like this, and improve it for yourself?" said Clarence. "All these valley terraces are bound to rise in value, and meantime you would be independent. It could be managed, Jim. I think *I* could arrange it for you," he went on, with a slight glow of youthful enthusiasm. "Write to me at Peyton's ranch, and I 'll see you when I come back, and we 'll hunt up something for you together." As Jim received the proposition with a kind of gloomy embarrassment, he added lightly, with a glance at the farmhouse, "It might be near *here,* you know; and you 'd have pleasant neighbors, and even eager listeners to your old adventures."

"You 'd better come in a minit before you go," said Jim, clumsily evading a direct reply. Clarence hesitated a moment, and then yielded. For an equal moment Jim Hooker was torn between secret jealousy of his old comrade's graces and a desire to present them as familiar associations of his own. But his vanity was quickly appeased.

Need it be said that the two women received this fleck and foam of a super-civiliza-
tion they knew little of as almost an imper-
tinence compared to the rugged, gloomy,
pathetic, and equally youthful hero of an
adventurous wilderness of which they knew
still less? What availed the courtesy and
gentle melancholy of Clarence Brant beside
the mysterious gloom and dark savagery of
Red Jim? Yet they received him patroniz-
ingly, as one who was, like themselves, an
admirer of manly grace and power, and the
recipient of Jim's friendship. The farmer
alone seemed to prefer Clarence, and yet
the latter's tacit indorsement of Red Jim,
through his evident previous intimacy with
him, impressed the man in Jim's favor.
All of which Clarence saw with that sensitive perception which had given him an
early insight into human weakness, yet still
had never shaken his youthful optimism.
He smiled a little thoughtfully, but was
openly fraternal to Jim, courteous to his
host and family, and, as he rode away in the
faint moonlight, magnificently opulent in
his largess to the farmer, — his first and
only assertion of his position.

The farmhouse, straggling barn, and

fringe of dusty willows, the white dome of
the motionless wagon, with the hanging
frying pans and kettles showing in the
moonlight like black silhouettes against the
staring canvas, all presently sank behind
Clarence like the details of a dream, and he
was alone with the moon, the hazy mystery
of the level, grassy plain, and the monotony
of the unending road. As he rode slowly
along he thought of that other dreary plain,
white with alkali patches and brown with
rings of deserted camp-fires, known to his
boyhood of deprivation, dependency, danger, and adventure, oddly enough, with a
strange delight; and his later years of study,
monastic seclusion, and final ease and independence, with an easy sense of wasted
existence and useless waiting. He remembered his homeless childhood in the South,
where servants and slaves took the place of
the father he had never known, and the
mother that he rarely saw; he remembered
his abandonment to a mysterious female
relation, where his natural guardians seemed
to have overlooked and forgotten him, until
he was sent, an all too young adventurer,
to work his passage on an overland emigrant
train across the plains; he remembered, as

yesterday, the fears, the hopes, the dreams
and dangers of that momentous journey. He
recalled his little playmate, Susy, and their
strange adventures — the whole incident that
the imaginative Jim Hooker had translated
and rehearsed as his own — rose vividly
before him. He thought of the cruel end
of that pilgrimage, which again left him
homeless and forgotten by even the relative
he was seeking in a strange land. He remembered his solitary journey to the gold
mines, taken with a boy's trust and a boy's
fearlessness, and the strange protector he
had found there, who had news of his missing kinsman; he remembered how this protector — whom he had at once instinctively
loved — transferred him to the house of this
new-found relation, who treated him kindly
and sent him to the Jesuit school, but who
never awakened in him a feeling of kinship.
He dreamed again of his life at school, his
accidental meeting with Susy at Santa Clara,
the keen revival of his boyish love for his
old playmate, now a pretty schoolgirl, the
petted adopted child of wealthy parents.
He recalled the terrible shock that interrupted this boyish episode: the news of the
death of his protector, and the revelation

that this hard, silent, and mysterious man was his own father, whose reckless life and desperate reputation had impelled him to assume a disguise.

He remembered how his sudden accession to wealth and independence had half frightened him, and had always left a lurking sensitiveness that he was unfairly favored, by some mere accident, above his less lucky companions. The rude vices of his old associates had made him impatient of the feebler sensual indulgences of the later companions of his luxury, and exposed their hollow fascinations; his sensitive fastidiousness kept him clean among vulgar temptations; his clear perceptions were never blinded by selfish sophistry. Meantime his feeling for Susy remained unchanged. Pride had kept him from seeking the Peytons. His present visit was as unpremeditated as Peyton's invitation had been unlooked for by him. Yet he had not allowed himself to be deceived. He knew that this courtesy was probably due to the change in his fortune, although he had hoped it might have been some change in their opinion brought about by Susy. But he would at least see her again, not in the pretty, half-clandestine way she had thought necessary, but openly and as her equal.

In his rapid ride he seemed to have suddenly penetrated the peaceful calm of the night. The restless irritation of the afternoon trade winds had subsided; the tender moonlight had hushed and tranquilly possessed the worried plain; the unending files of wild oats, far spaced and distinct, stood erect and motionless as trees; something of the sedate solemnity of a great forest seemed to have fallen upon their giant stalks. There was no dew. In that light, dry air, the heavier dust no longer rose beneath the heels of his horse, whose flying shadow passed over the field like a cloud, leaving no trail or track behind it. In the preoccupation of his thought and his breathless retrospect, the young man had ridden faster than he intended, and he now checked his panting horse. The influence of the night and the hushed landscape stole over him; his thoughts took a gentler turn; in that dim, mysterious horizon line before him, his future seemed to be dreamily peopled with airy, graceful shapes that more or less took the likeness of Susy. She was bright, coquettish, romantic, as he had last seen her;

she was older, graver, and thoughtfully welcome of him; or she was cold, distant, and
severely forgetful of the past.   How would
her adopted father and mother receive him?
Would they ever look upon him in the light
of a suitor to the young girl?   He had no
fear of Peyton, — he understood his own sex,
and, young as he was, knew already how to
make himself respected; but how could he
overcome that instinctive aversion which
Mrs. Peyton had so often made him feel he
had provoked?   Yet in this dreamy hush
of earth and sky, what was not possible?
His boyish heart beat high with daring visions.

He saw Mrs. Peyton in the porch, wel-
coming him with that maternal smile which
his childish longing had so often craved to
share with Susy.   Peyton would be there,
too, — Peyton, who had once pushed back
his torn straw hat to look approvingly in
his boyish eyes; and Peyton, perhaps, might
be proud of him.

Suddenly he started.   A voice in his very
ear!

"Bah!   A yoke of vulgar cattle grazing
on lands that were thine by right and law.
Neither more nor less than that.   And I

tell thee, Pancho, like cattle, to be driven
off or caught and branded for one's own.
Ha! There are those who could swear to
the truth of this on the Creed. Ay! and
bring papers stamped and signed by the
governor's rubric to prove it. And not
that I hate them, — bah! what are those
heretic swine to me? But thou dost comprehend me? It galls and pricks me to see
them swelling themselves with stolen husks,
and men like thee, Pancho, ousted from
their own land."

Clarence had halted in utter bewilder-
ment. No one was visible before him, behind him, on either side. The words, in
Spanish, came from the air, the sky, the
distant horizon, he knew not which. Was
he still dreaming? A strange shiver crept
over his skin as if the air had grown suddenly chill. Then another mysterious voice
arose, incredulous, half mocking, but
equally distinct and clear.

"Caramba! What is this? You are
wandering, friend Pancho. You are still
smarting from his tongue. He has the
grant confirmed by his brigand government;
he has the *possession*, stolen by a thief like
himself; and he has the Corregidors with

him. For is he not one of them himself, this Judge Peyton?"

Peyton! Clarence felt the blood rush back to his face in astonishment and indignation. His heels mechanically pressed his horse's 'flanks, and the animal sprang forward.

"*Guarda! Mira!*" said the voice again in a quicker, lower tone. But this time it was evidently in the field beside him, and the heads and shoulders of two horsemen emerged at the same moment from the tall ranks of wild oats. The mystery was solved. The strangers had been making their way along a lower level of the terraced plain, hidden by the grain, not twenty yards away, and parallel with the road they were now ascending to join. Their figures were alike formless in long striped *serapes*, and their features undistinguishable under stiff black sombreros.

"*Buenas noches*, señor," said the second voice, in formal and cautious deliberation.

A sudden inspiration made Clarence respond in English, as if he had not comprehended the stranger's words, "Eh?"

"Gooda-nighta," repeated the stranger.

"Oh, good-night," returned Clarence.

They passed him. Their spurs tinkled twice or thrice, their mustangs sprang forward, and the next moment the loose folds of their *serapes* were fluttering at their sides like wings in their flight.

CHAPTER IV.

AFTER the chill of a dewless night the morning sun was apt to look ardently upon the Robles Rancho, if so strong an expression could describe the dry, oven-like heat of a Californian coast-range valley. Before ten o'clock the adobe wall of the *patio* was warm enough to permit lingering vacqueros and idle *peons* to lean against it, and the exposed *annexe* was filled with sharp, resinous odors from the oozing sap of unseasoned "redwood" boards, warped and drying in the hot sunshine. Even at that early hour the climbing Castilian roses were drooping against the wooden columns of the new veranda, scarcely older than themselves, and mingling an already faded spice with the aroma of baking wood and the more material fragrance of steaming coffee, that seemed dominant everywhere.

In fact, the pretty breakfast-room, whose three broad windows, always open to the veranda, gave an *al fresco* effect to every

meal, was a pathetic endeavor of the South-
ern-bred Peyton to emulate the soft, luxu-
rious, and open-air indolence of his native
South, in a climate that was not only *not*
tropical, but even austere in its most fervid
moments. Yet, although cold draughts invaded it from the rear that morning, Judge
Peyton sat alone, between the open doors
and windows, awaiting the slow coming of
his wife and the young ladies. He was not
in an entirely comfortable mood that morning. Things were not going on well at
Robles. That truculent vagabond, Pedro,
had, the night before, taken himself off with
a curse that had frightened even the vacqueros, who most hated him as a companion,
but who now seemed inclined to regard his
absence as an injury done to their race.
Peyton, uneasily conscious that his own
anger had been excited by an exaggerated
conception of the accident, was now, like
most obstinate men, inclined to exaggerate
the importance of Pedro's insolence. He
was well out of it to get rid of this quarrel-
some hanger-on, whose presumption and ill-
humor threatened the discipline of the
rancho, yet he could not entirely forget that
he had employed him on account of his fam-

ily claims, and from a desire to placate racial jealousy and settle local differences. For the inferior Mexicans and Indian half-breeds still regarded their old masters with affection; were, in fact, more concerned for the integrity of their caste than the masters were themselves, and the old Spanish families who had made alliances with Americans, and shared their land with them, had rarely succeeded in alienating their retainers with their lands. Certain experiences in the proving of his grant before the Land Commission had taught Peyton that they were not to be depended upon. And lately there had been unpleasant rumors of the discovery of some unlooked-for claimants to a division of the grant itself, which might affect his own title.

He looked up quickly as voices and light steps on the veranda at last heralded the approach of his tardy household from the corridor. But, in spite of his preoccupation, he was startled and even awkwardly impressed with a change in Susy's appearance. She was wearing, for the first time, a long skirt, and this sudden maturing of her figure struck him, as a man, much more forcibly than it would probably have im-

pressed a woman, more familiar with details. He had not noticed ·certain indications of womanhood, as significant, perhaps,
in her carriage as her outlines, which had
been lately perfectly apparent to her mother
and Mary, but which were to him now, for
the first time, indicated by a few inches of
skirt. She not only looked taller to his
masculine eyes, but these few inches had
added to the mystery as well as the drapery
of the goddess; they were not so much the
revelation of maturity as the suggestion that
it was *hidden*. So impressed was he, that a
half-serious lecture on her yesterday's child-
ishness, the outcome of his irritated reflec-
tions that morning, died upon his lips. He
felt he was no longer dealing with a child.

He welcomed them with that smile of
bantering approbation, supposed to keep
down inordinate vanity, which for some
occult reason one always reserves for the
members of one's own family. He was
quite conscious that Susy was looking very
pretty in this new and mature frock, and
that as she stood beside his wife, far from
ageing Mrs. Peyton's good looks and figure,
she appeared like an equal companion, and
that they mutually "became" one another.

This, and the fact that they were all, including Mary Rogers, in their freshest, gayest morning dresses, awakened a half-humorous, half-real apprehension in his mind, that he was now hopelessly surrounded by a matured sex, and in a weak minority.

"I think I ought to have been prepared," he began grimly, "for this addition to — to — the skirts of my family."

"Why, John," returned Mrs. Peyton quickly; "do you mean to say you haven't noticed that the poor child has for weeks been looking positively indecent?"

"Really, papa, I've been a sight to behold. Haven't I, Mary?" chimed in Susy.

"Yes, dear. Why, Judge, I've been wondering that Susy stood it so well, and never complained."

Peyton glanced around him at this compact feminine embattlement. It was as he feared. Yet even here he was again at fault.

"And," said Mrs. Peyton slowly, with the reserved significance of the feminine postscript in her voice, "if that Mr. Brant is coming here to-day, it would be just as well for him to see *that she is no longer a child, as when he knew her.*"

An hour later, good-natured Mary Rogers, in her character of "a dear," — which
was usually indicated by the undertaking of
small errands for her friend, — was gathering roses from the old garden for Susy's
adornment, when she saw a vision which lingered with her for many a day. She had
stopped to look through the iron *grille* in
the adobe wall, across the open wind-swept
plain. Miniature waves were passing over
the wild oats, with glittering disturbances
here and there in the depressions like the
sparkling of green foam; the horizon line
was sharply defined against the hard, steel-
blue sky; everywhere the brand-new morning was shining with almost painted brilliancy; the vigor, spirit, and even crudeness
of youth were over all. The young girl
was dazzled and bewildered. Suddenly, as
if blown out of the waving grain, or an in-
carnation of the vivid morning, the bright
and striking figure of a youthful horseman
flashed before the *grille.* It was Clarence
Brant! Mary Rogers had always seen him,
in the loyalty of friendship, with Susy's
prepossessed eyes, yet she fancied that
morning that he had never looked so handsome before. Even the foppish fripperies

of his riding-dress and silver trappings seemed as much the natural expression of conquering youth as the invincible morning sunshine. Perhaps it might have been a reaction against Susy's caprice or some latent susceptibility of her own; but a momentary antagonism to her friend stirred even her kindly nature. What right had Susy to trifle with such an opportunity? Who was *she* to hesitate over this gallant prince?

But Prince Charming's quick eyes had detected her, and the next moment his beautiful horse was beside the grating, and his ready hand of greeting extended through the bars.

"I suppose I am early and unexpected, but I slept at Santa Inez last night, that I might ride over in the cool of the morning. My things are coming by the stage-coach, later. It seemed such a slow way of coming one's self."

Mary Rogers's black eyes intimated that the way he had taken was the right one, but she gallantly recovered herself and remembered her position as confidante. And here was the opportunity of delivering Susy's warning unobserved. She withdrew her hand from Clarence's frank grasp, and pass-

ing it through the grating, patted the sleek,
shining flanks of his horse, with a discreet
division of admiration.

"And such a lovely creature, too! And
Susy will be so delighted! and oh, Mr.
Brant, please, you 're to say nothing of
having met her at Santa Clara. It 's just
as well not to begin with *that* here, for, you
see " (with a large, maternal manner), "you
were both *so* young then."

Clarence drew a quick breath. It was
the first check to his vision of independence
and equal footing! Then his invitation was
not the outcome of a continuous friendship
revived by Susy, as he had hoped; the Peytons had known nothing of his meeting with
her, or perhaps they would not have invited
him. He was here as an impostor, — and all
because Susy had chosen to make a mystery
of a harmless encounter, which might have
been explained, and which they might have
even countenanced. He thought bitterly of
his old playmate for a brief moment, — as
brief as Mary's antagonism. The young
girl noticed the change in his face, but misinterpreted it.

"Oh, there 's no danger of its coming out
if you don't say anything," she said,

quickly. "Ride on to the house, and don't wait for me. You 'll find them in the *patio* on the veranda."

Clarence moved on, but not as spiritedly as before. Nevertheless there was still dash enough about him and the animal he bestrode to stir into admiration the few lounging vacqueros of a country which was apt to judge the status of a rider by the quality of his horse. Nor was the favorable impression confined to them alone. Peyton's gratification rang out cheerily in his greeting : —

"Bravo, Clarence! You are here in true *caballero* style. Thanks for the compliment to the rancho."

For a moment the young man was transported back again to his boyhood, and once more felt Peyton's approving hand pushing back the worn straw hat from his childish forehead. A faint color rose to his cheeks; his eyes momentarily dropped. The highest art could have done no more! The slight aggressiveness of his youthful finery and picturesque good looks was condoned at once; his modesty conquered where self-assertion might have provoked opposition, and even Mrs. Peyton felt herself impelled to come forward with an outstretched hand scarcely less frank than her husband's. Then Clarence lifted his eyes. He saw before him the woman to whom his childish heart had gone out with the inscrutable longing and adoration of a motherless, homeless, companionless boy; the woman who had absorbed the love of his playmate without sharing it with him; who had showered her protecting and maternal caresses on Susy, a waif like himself, yet had not only left his heart lonely and desolate, but had even added to his childish distrust of himself the thought that he had excited her aversion. He saw her more beautiful than ever in her restored health, freshness of coloring, and mature roundness of outline. He was unconsciously touched with a man's admiration for her without losing his boyish yearnings and half-filial affection; in her new materialistic womanhood his youthful imagination had lifted her to a queen and goddess. There was all this appeal in his still boyish eyes, — eyes that had never yet known shame or fear in the expression of their emotions; there was all this in the gesture with which he lifted Mrs. Peyton's fingers to his lips. The little

group saw in this act only a Spanish courtesy in keeping with his accepted rôle. But
a thrill of surprise, of embarrassment, of
intense gratification passed over her. For
he had not even looked at Susy!

Her relenting was graceful. She welcomed him with a winning smile. Then
she motioned pleasantly towards Susy.

"But here is an older friend, Mr. Brant,
whom you do not seem to recognize, —
Susy, whom you have not seen since she
was a child."

A quick flush rose to Clarence's cheek.
The group smiled at this evident youthful
confession of some boyish admiration. But
Clarence knew that his truthful blood was
merely resenting the deceit his lips were
sealed from divulging. He did not dare to
glance at Susy; it added to the general amuse-
ment that the young girl was obliged to present herself. But in this interval she had
exchanged glances with Mary Rogers, who
had rejoined the group, and she knew she
was safe. She smiled with gracious conde-
scension at Clarence; observed, with the
patronizing superiority of age and established position, that he had *grown,* but had
not greatly changed, and, it is needless to

say, again filled her mother's heart with
joy. Clarence, still intoxicated with Mrs.
Peyton's kindliness, and, perhaps, still embarrassed by remorse, had not time to remark the girl's studied attitude. He shook
hands with her cordially, and then, in the
quick reaction of youth, accepted with hu-
morous gravity the elaborate introduction to
Mary Rogers by Susy, which completed this
little comedy. And if, with a woman's
quickness, Mrs. Peyton detected a certain
lingering glance which passed between Mary
Rogers and Clarence, and misinterpreted it,
it was only a part of that mystification into
which these youthful actors are apt to throw
their mature audiences.

"Confess, Ally," said Peyton, cheerfully,
as the three young people suddenly found
their tongues with aimless vivacity and inconsequent laughter, and started with unin-
telligible spirits for an exploration of the
garden, "confess now that your *bête noir* is
really a very manly as well as a very pre-
sentable young fellow. By Jove! the *padres*
have made a Spanish swell out of him without spoiling the Brant grit, either! Come,
now; you're not afraid that Susy's style
will suffer from *his* companionship. 'Pon

my soul, she might borrow a little of his
courtesy to his elders without indelicacy.
I only wish she had as sincere a way of
showing her respect for you as he has. Did
you notice that he really did n't seem to see
anybody else but you at first? And yet
you never were a friend to him, like Susy."

The lady tossed her head slightly, but
smiled.

"This is the first time he's seen Mary
Rogers, is n't it?" she said meditatively.

"I reckon. But what's that to do with
his politeness to you?"

"And do her parents know him?" she
continued, without replying.

"How do I know? I suppose everybody
has heard of him. Why?"

"Because I think they've taken a fancy
to each other."

"What in the name of folly, Ally"—
began the despairing Peyton.

"When you invite a handsome, rich, and
fascinating young man into the company of
young ladies, John," returned Mrs. Peyton,
in her severest manner, "you must not forget you owe a certain responsibility to the
parents. I shall certainly look after Miss
Rogers."

CHAPTER V.

ALTHOUGH the three young people had left the veranda together, when they reached the old garden Clarence and Susy found themselves considerably in advance of Mary Rogers, who had become suddenly and deeply interested in the beauty of a passion vine near the gate. At the first discovery of their isolation their voluble exchange of information about themselves and their occupations since their last meeting stopped simultaneously. Clarence, who had forgotten his momentary irritation, and had recovered his old happiness in her presence, was nevertheless conscious of some other change in her than that suggested by the lengthened skirt and the later and more delicate accentuation of her prettiness. It was not her affectation of superiority and older social experience, for that was only the outcome of what he had found charming in her as a child, and which he still good-humoredly accepted; nor was it her characteristic exaggeration of speech, which he still pleasantly recognized. It was something else, vague and indefinite, — something that had been unnoticed while Mary was with them, but had now come between them like some unknown presence which had taken the confidante's place. He remained silent, looking at her half-brightening cheek and conscious profile. Then he spoke with awkward directness.

"You are changed, Susy, more than in looks."

"Hush," said the girl in a tragic whisper, with a warning gesture towards the blandly unconscious Mary.

"But," returned Clarence wonderingly, "she's your — our friend, you know."

"I *don't* know," said Susy, in a still deeper tone, "that is — oh, don't ask me! But when you're always surrounded by spies, when you can't say your soul is your own, you doubt everybody!" There was such a pretty distress in her violet eyes and curving eyebrows, that Clarence, albeit vague as to its origin and particulars, nevertheless possessed himself of the little hand that was gesticulating dangerously near his own, and pressed it sympathetically. Perhaps preoccupied with her emotions, she did not immediately withdraw it, as she went on rapidly: "And if you were cooped up here, day after day, behind these bars," pointing to the *grille*, "you 'd know what I suffer."

"But " — began Clarence.

"Hush!" said Susy, with a stamp of her little foot.

Clarence, who had only wished to point out that the whole lower end of the garden wall was in ruins and the *grille* really was no prevention, " hushed."

"And listen! Don't pay me much attention to-day, but talk to *her*," indicating the still discreet and distant Mary, "before father and mother. Not a word to her of this confidence, Clarence. To-morrow ride out alone on your beautiful horse, and come back by way of the woods, beyond our turning, at four o'clock. There 's a trail to the right of the big *madroño* tree. Take that. Be careful and keep a good lookout, for she must n't see you."

"Who must n't see me?" said the puzzled Clarence.

"Why, Mary, of course, you silly boy!" returned the girl impatiently. "She 'll be

looking for *me*. Go now, Clarence! Stop!
Look at that lovely big maiden's-blush up
there," pointing to a pink-suffused speci-
men of rose *grandiflora* hanging on the wall.
"Get it, Clarence, — that one, — I 'll show
you where, — there!" They had already
plunged into the leafy bramble, and, standing on tiptoe, with her hand on his shoulder
and head upturned, Susy's cheek had innocently approached Clarence's own. At this
moment Clarence, possibly through some
confusion of color, fragrance, or softness of
contact, seemed to have availed himself of
the opportunity, in a way which caused Susy
to instantly rejoin Mary Rogers with affected
dignity, leaving him to follow a few moments later with the captured flower.

Without trying to understand the reason
of to-morrow's rendezvous, and perhaps not
altogether convinced of the reality of Susy's
troubles, he, however, did not find that difficulty in carrying out her other commands
which he had expected. Mrs. Peyton was
still gracious, and, with feminine tact, in-
duced him to talk of himself, until she was
presently in possession of his whole history,
barring the episode of his meeting with Susy,
since he had parted with them. He felt a

strange satisfaction in familiarly pouring
out his confidences to this superior woman,
whom he had always held in awe. There
was a new delight in her womanly interest
in his trials and adventures, and a subtle
pleasure even in her half-motherly criticism
and admonition of some passages. I am
afraid he forgot Susy, who listened with the
complacency of an exhibitor; Mary, whose
black eyes dilated alternately with sympathy
for the performer and deprecation of Mrs.
Peyton's critical glances; and Peyton, who,
however, seemed lost in thought, and preoccupied. Clarence was happy. The softly
shaded lights in the broad, spacious, comfortably furnished drawing-room shone on
the group before him. It was a picture of
refined domesticity which the homeless Clarence had never known except as a vague,
half-painful, boyish remembrance; it was a
realization of welcome that far exceeded his
wildest boyish vision of the preceding night.
With that recollection came another, — a
more uneasy one. He remembered how that
vision had been interrupted by the strange
voices in the road, and their vague but
ominous import to his host. A feeling of
self-reproach came over him. The threats

had impressed him as only mere braggadocio, — he knew the characteristic exaggeration of the race, — but perhaps he ought
to privately tell Peyton of the incident at
once.

The opportunity came later, when the
ladies had retired, and Peyton, wrapped in
a *poncho* in a rocking-chair, on the now
chilly veranda, looked up from his reverie
and a cigar. Clarence casually introduced
the incident, as if only for the sake of de-
scribing the supernatural effect of the hidden voices, but he was concerned to see
that Peyton was considerably disturbed by
their more material import. After questioning him as to the appearance of the two
men, his host said: "I don't mind telling
you, Clarence, that as far as that fellow's
intentions go he is quite sincere, although
his threats are only borrowed thunder. He
is a man whom I have just dismissed for
carelessness and insolence, — two things
that run in double harness in this country,
— but I should be more afraid to find him
at my back on a dark night, alone on the
plains, than to confront him in daylight, in
the witness box, against me. He was only
repeating a silly rumor that the title to this

rancho and the nine square leagues beyond
would be attacked by some speculators."

"But I thought your title was confirmed
two years ago," said Clarence.

"The *grant* was confirmed," returned
Peyton, "which means that the conveyance
of the Mexican government of these lands
to the ancestor of Victor Robles was held
to be legally proven by the United States
Land Commission, and a patent issued to
all those who held under it. I and my
neighbors hold under it by purchase from
Victor Robles, subject to the confirmation
of the Land Commission. But that confirmation was only of Victor's *great-grand-
father's title*, and it is now alleged that as
Victor's father died without making a will,
Victor has claimed and disposed of property
which he ought to have divided with his *sisters*. At least, some speculating rascals in
San Francisco have set up what they call
'the Sisters' title,' and are selling it to actual settlers on the unoccupied lands beyond.
As, by the law, it would hold possession
against the mere ordinary squatters, whose
only right is based, as you know, on the
presumption that there is *no title claimed*,
it gives the possessor immunity to enjoy the

use of the property until the case is decided,
and even should the original title hold good
against his, the successful litigant would
probably be willing to pay for improvements and possession to save the expensive
and tedious process of ejectment."

"But this does not affect *you*, who have
already possession?" said Clarence quickly.

"No, not as far as *this house* and the
lands I actually *occupy and cultivate* are
concerned; and they know that I am safe to
fight to the last, and carry the case to the
Supreme Court in that case, until the swin-
dle is exposed, or they drop it; but I may
have to pay them something to keep the
squatters off my *unoccupied* land."

"But you surely would n't recognize those
rascals in any way?" said the astonished
Clarence.

"As against other rascals? Why not?"
returned Peyton grimly. "I only pay for
the possession which their sham title gives
me to my own land. If by accident that
title obtains, I am still on the safe side."
After a pause he said, more gravely, "What
you overheard, Clarence, shows me that the
plan is more forward than I had imagined,
and that I may have to fight traitors here."

"I hope, sir," said Clarence, with a quick glow in his earnest face, "that you'll let me help you. You thought I did once, you remember, — with the Indians."

There was so much of the old Clarence in his boyish appeal and eager, questioning face that Peyton, who had been talking to him as a younger but equal man of affairs, was startled into a smile. "You did, Clarence, though the Indians butchered your friends, after all. I don't know, though, but that your experiences with those Spaniards — you must have known a lot of them when you were with Don Juan Robinson and at the college — might be of service in getting at evidence, or smashing their witnesses if it comes to a fight. But just now, *money* is everything. They must be bought *off the land* if I have to mortgage it for the purpose. That strikes you as a rather heroic remedy, Clarence, eh?" he continued, in his old, half-bantering attitude towards Clarence's inexperienced youth, "don't it?"

But Clarence was not thinking of that. Another more audacious but equally youthful and enthusiastic idea had taken possession of his mind, and he lay awake half that night revolving it. It was true that it was

somewhat impractically mixed with his
visions of Mrs. Peyton and Susy, and even
included his previous scheme of relief for
the improvident and incorrigible Hooker.
But it gave a wonderful sincerity and happiness to his slumbers that night, which the
wiser and elder Peyton might have envied,
and I wot not was in the long run as correct
and sagacious as Peyton's sleepless cogita-
tions. And in the early morning Mr. Clarence Brant, the young capitalist, sat down
to his traveling-desk and wrote two clear-
headed, logical, and practical business letters, — one to his banker, and the other to
his former guardian, Don Juan Robinson, —
as his first step in a resolve that was, nevertheless, perhaps as wildly quixotic and
enthusiastic as any dream his boyish and
unselfish heart had ever indulged.

At breakfast, in the charmed freedom of
the domestic circle, Clarence forgot Susy's
capricious commands of yesterday, and began to address himself to her in his old earnest fashion, until he was warned by a significant knitting of the young lady's brows
and monosyllabic responses. But in his
youthful loyalty to Mrs. Peyton, he was
more pained to notice Susy's occasional un-

conscious indifference to her adopted mother's affectionate expression, and a more
conscious disregard of her wishes. So
uneasy did he become, in his sensitive concern for Mrs. Peyton's half-concealed mortification, that he gladly accepted Peyton's
offer to go with him to visit the farm and
corral. As the afternoon approached, with
another twinge of self - reproach, he was
obliged to invent some excuse to decline
certain hospitable plans of Mrs. Peyton's
for his entertainment, and at half past three
stole somewhat guiltily, with his horse, from
the stables. But he had to pass before the
outer wall of the garden and *grille*, through
which he had seen Mary the day before.
Raising his eyes mechanically, he was startled to see Mrs. Peyton standing behind the
grating, with her abstracted gaze fixed upon
the wind - tossed, level grain beyond her.
She smiled as she saw him, but there were
traces of tears in her proud, handsome eyes.

"You are going to ride?" she said pleasantly.

"Y-e-es," stammered the shamefaced
Clarence.

She glanced at him wistfully.

"You are right. The girls have gone

away by themselves. Mr. Peyton has ridden
over to Santa Inez on this dreadful land
business, and I suppose you'd have found
him a dull riding companion. It is rather
stupid here. I quite envy you, Mr. Brant,
your horse and your freedom."

"But, Mrs. Peyton," broke in Clarence,
impulsively, "you have a horse — I saw it, a
lovely lady's horse — eating its head off in
the stable. Won't you let me run back and
order it; and won't you, please, come out
with me for a good, long gallop?"

He meant what he said. He had spoken
quickly, impulsively, but with the perfect
understanding in his own mind that his
proposition meant the complete abandonment of his rendezvous with Susy. Mrs.
Peyton was astounded and slightly stirred
with his earnestness, albeit unaware of all
it implied.

"It's a great temptation, Mr. Brant,"
she said, with a playful smile, which dazzled
Clarence with its first faint suggestion of a
refined woman's coquetry; "but I'm afraid
that Mr. Peyton would think me going mad
in my old age. No. Go on and enjoy your
gallop, and if you should see those giddy
girls anywhere, send them home early for
chocolate, before the cold wind gets up."

She turned, waved her slim white hand
playfully in acknowledgment of Clarence's
bared head, and moved away.

For the first few moments the young man
tried to find relief in furious riding, and in
bullying his spirited horse. Then he pulled
quickly up. What was he doing? What
was he going to do? What foolish, vapid
deceit was this that he was going to practice
upon that noble, queenly, confiding, gener-
ous woman? (He had already forgotten
that she had always distrusted him.) What
a fool he was not to tell her half-jokingly
that he expected to meet Susy! But would
he have dared to talk half-jokingly to such
a woman on such a topic? And would it
have been honorable without disclosing the
whole truth, — that they had met secretly
before? And was it fair to Susy? — dear,
innocent, childish Susy! Yet something
must be done! It was such trivial, pur-
poseless deceit, after all; for this noble
woman, Mrs. Peyton, so kind, so gentle,
would never object to his loving Susy and
marrying her. And they would all live
happily together; and Mrs. Peyton would
never be separated from them, but always
beaming tenderly upon them as she did just

now in the garden. Yes, he would have a
serious understanding with Susy, and that
would excuse the clandestine meeting to-day.

His rapid pace, meantime, had brought
him to the imperceptible incline of the terrace, and he was astonished, in turning in
the saddle, to find that the *casa*, corral, and
outbuildings had completely vanished, and
that behind him rolled only the long sea of
grain, which seemed to have swallowed them
in its yellowing depths. Before him lay
the wooded ravine through which the stage-
coach passed, which was also the entrance to
the rancho, and there, too, probably, was the
turning of which Susy had spoken. But it
was still early for the rendezvous; indeed,
he was in no hurry to meet her in his present discontented state, and he made a listless circuit of the field, in the hope of dis-
covering the phenomena that had caused the
rancho's mysterious disappearance. When
he had found that it was the effect of the
different levels, his attention was arrested
by a multitude of moving objects in a still
more distant field, which proved to be a
band of wild horses. In and out among
them, circling aimlessly, as it seemed to
him, appeared two horsemen apparently

performing some mystic evolution. To add
to their singular performance, from time to
time one of the flying herd, driven by the
horsemen far beyond the circle of its companions, dropped suddenly and unaccount-
ably in full career. The field closed over
it as if it had been swallowed up. In a few
moments it appeared again, trotting peacefully behind its former pursuer. It was some
time before Clarence grasped the meaning
of this strange spectacle. Although the
clear, dry atmosphere sharply accented the
silhouette - like outlines of the men and
horses, so great was the distance that the
slender forty-foot lasso, which in the skill-
ful hands of the horsemen had effected these
captures, was *completely invisible!* The
horsemen were Peyton's vacqueros, making
a selection from the young horses for the
market. He remembered now that Peyton
had told him that he might be obliged to
raise money by sacrificing some of his stock,
and the thought brought back Clarence's uneasiness as he turned again to the trail. Indeed, he was hardly in the vein for a gentle
tryst, as he entered the wooded ravine to
seek the *madroño* tree which was to serve
as a guide to his lady's bower.

A few rods further, under the cool vault
filled with woodland spicing, he came upon
it. In its summer harlequin dress of scarlet and green, with hanging bells of poly-
tinted berries, like some personified sylvan
Folly, it seemed a fitting symbol of Susy's
childish masquerade of passion. Its bizarre
beauty, so opposed to the sober gravity of
the sedate pines and hemlocks, made it
an unmistakable landmark. Here he dismounted and picketed his horse. And here,
beside it, to the right, ran the little trail
crawling over mossy boulders; a narrow
yellow track through the carpet of pine
needles between the closest file of trees; an
almost imperceptible streak across pools of
chickweed at their roots, and a brown and
ragged swath through the ferns. As he
went on, the anxiety and uneasiness that had
possessed him gave way to a languid intoxi-
cation of the senses; the mysterious seclusion of these woodland depths recovered the
old influence they had exerted over his boyhood. He was not returning to Susy, as
much as to the older love of his youth, of
which she was, perhaps, only an incident.
It was therefore with an odd boyish thrill
again that, coming suddenly upon a little

hollow, like a deserted nest, where the lost trail made him hesitate, he heard the crackle of a starched skirt behind him, was conscious of the subtle odor of freshly ironed and scented muslin, and felt the gentle pressure of delicate fingers upon his eyes.

"Susy!"

"You silly boy! Where were you blundering to? Why didn't you look around you?"

"I thought I would hear your voices."

"Whose voices, idiot?"

"Yours and Mary's," returned Clarence innocently, looking round for the confidante.

"Oh, indeed! Then you wanted to see *Mary?* Well, she's looking for me somewhere. Perhaps you'll go and find her, or shall I?"

She was offering to pass him when he laid his hand on hers to detain her. She instantly evaded it, and drew herself up to her full height, incontestably displaying the dignity of the added inches to her skirt. All this was charmingly like the old Susy, but it did not bid fair to help him to a serious interview. And, looking at the pretty, pink, mocking face before him, with the witchery of the woodland still upon him,

he began to think that he had better put
it off.

"Never mind about Mary," he said laugh-
ingly. "But you said you wanted to see
me, Susy; and here I am."

"Said I wanted to see you?" repeated
Susy, with her blue eyes lifted in celestial
scorn and wonderment. "Said *I* wanted
to see you? Are you not mistaken, Mr.
Brant? Really, I imagined that you came
here to see *me*."

With her fair head upturned, and the leaf
of her scarlet lip temptingly curled over,
Clarence began to think this latest phase of
her extravagance the most fascinating. He
drew nearer to her as he said gently, "You
know what I mean, Susy. You said yesterday you were troubled. I thought you
might have something to tell me."

"I should think it was *you* who might
have something to tell me after all these
years," she said poutingly, yet self-pos-
sessed. "But I suppose you came here only
to see Mary and mother. I 'm sure you let
them know that plainly enough last evening."

"But you said" — began the stupefied
Clarence.

"Never mind what *I* said. It's always what *I* say, never what *you* say; and you don't say anything."

The woodland influence must have been still very strong upon Clarence that he did not discover in all this that, while Susy's general capriciousness was unchanged, there was a new and singular insincerity in her manifest acting. She was either concealing the existence of some other real emotion, or assuming one that was absent. But he did not notice it, and only replied tenderly: —

"But I want to say a great deal to you, Susy. I want to say that if you still feel as I do, and as I have always felt, and you think you could be happy as *I* would be if — if — we could be always together, we need not conceal it from your mother and father any longer. I am old enough to speak for myself, and I am my own master. Your mother has been very kind to me, — so kind that it doesn't seem quite right to deceive her, — and when I tell her that I love you, and that I want you to be my wife, I believe she will give us her blessing."

Susy uttered a strange little laugh, and with an assumption of coyness, that was,

however, still affected, stooped to pick a few
berries from a *manzanita* bush.

"I 'll tell you what she 'll say, Clarence.
She 'll say you 're frightfully young, and so
you are!"

The young fellow tried to echo the laugh,
but felt as if he had received a blow. For
the first time he was conscious of the truth:
this girl, whom he had fondly regarded as
a child, had already passed him in the race;
she had become a woman before he was yet
a man, and now stood before him, maturer
in her knowledge, and older in her understanding, of herself and of him. This was
the change that had perplexed him; this was
the presence that had come between them,
— a Susy he had never known before.

She laughed at his changed expression,
and then swung herself easily to a sitting
posture on the low projecting branch of a
hemlock. The act was still girlish, but,
nevertheless, she looked down upon him in
a superior, patronizing way. "Now, Clarence," she said, with a half-abstracted manner, "don't you be a big fool! If you talk
that way to mother, she 'll only tell you to
wait two or three years until you know
your own mind, and she 'll pack me off to

that horrid school again, besides watching
me like a cat every moment you are here.
If you want to stay here, and see me sometimes like this, you 'll just behave as you
have done, and say nothing. Do you see?
Perhaps you don't care to come, or are satisfied with Mary and mother. Say so, then.
Goodness knows, I don't want to force you
to come here."

Modest and reserved as Clarence was
generally, I fear that bashfulness of approach to the other sex was not one of these
indications. He walked up to Susy with
appalling directness, and passed his arm
around her waist. She did not move, but
remained looking at him and his intruding
arm with a certain critical curiosity, as if
awaiting some novel sensation. At which
he kissed her. She then slowly disengaged
his arm, and said: —

"Really, upon my word, Clarence," in
perfectly level tones, and slipped quietly to
the ground.

He again caught her in his arms, encir-
cling her disarranged hair and part of the
beribboned hat hanging over her shoulder, and remained for an instant holding
her thus silently and tenderly. Then she

freed herself with an abstracted air, a half
smile, and an unchanged color except where
her soft cheek had been abraded by his coat
collar.

"You 're a bold, rude boy, Clarence,"
she said, putting back her hair quietly, and
straightening the brim of her hat. "Heaven
knows where you learned manners!" and
then, from a safer distance, with the same
critical look in her violet eyes, "I suppose
you think mother would allow *that* if she
knew it?"

But Clarence, now completely subjugated,
with the memory of the kiss upon him and
a heightened color, protested that he only
wanted to make their intercourse less constrained, and to have their relations, even
their engagement, recognized by her parents; still he would take her advice. Only
there was always the danger that if they
were discovered she would be sent back to
the convent all the same, and his banish-
ment, instead of being the probation of a
few years, would be a perpetual separation.

"We could always run away, Clarence,"
responded the young girl calmly. "There 's
nothing the matter with *that.*"

Clarence was startled. The idea of deso-

lating the sad, proud, handsome Mrs. Peyton, whom he worshiped, and her kind husband, whom he was just about to serve, was
so grotesque and confusing, that he said
hopelessly, "Yes."

"Of course," she continued, with the
same odd affectation of coyness, which was,
however, distinctly uncalled for, as she eyed
him from under her broad hat, "you need n't
come with me unless you like. I can run
away by myself, — if I want to! I 've
thought of it before. One can't stand
everything!"

"But, Susy," said Clarence, with a swift
remorseful recollection of her confidence
yesterday, "is there really anything troubles you? Tell me, dear. What is it?"

"Oh, nothing — *everything!* It 's no
use, — *you* can't understand! *You* like it, I
know you do. I can see it; it 's your style.
But it 's stupid, it 's awful, Clarence!
With mamma snooping over you and around
you all day, with her 'dear child,' 'mamma's pet,' and 'What is it, dear?' and 'Tell
it all to your own mamma,' — as if I would!
And 'my own mamma,' indeed! As if I
did n't know, Clarence, that she *is n't.*
And papa, caring for nothing but this hid-

eous, dreary rancho, and the huge, empty plains. It's worse than school, for there, at least, when you went out, you could see something besides cattle and horses and yellow-faced half-breeds! But here — Lord! it's only a wonder I haven't run away before!"

Startled and shocked as Clarence was at this revelation, accompanied as it was by a hardness of manner that was new to him, the influence of the young girl was still so strong upon him that he tried to evade it as only an extravagance, and said with a faint smile, "But where would you run to?"

She looked at him cunningly, with her head on one side, and then said: —

"I have friends, and " —

She hesitated, pursing up her pretty lips.

"And what?"

"Relations."

"Relations?"

"Yes, — an aunt by marriage. She lives in Sacramento. She'd be overjoyed to have me come to her. Her second husband has a theatre there."

"But, Susy, what does Mrs. Peyton know of this?"

"Nothing. Do you think I'd tell her, and have her buy them up as she has my other relations? Do you suppose I don't know that I've been bought up like a nigger?"

She looked indignant, compressing her delicate little nostrils, and yet, somehow, Clarence had the same singular impression that she was only acting.

The calling of a far-off voice came faintly through the wood.

"That's Mary, looking for me," said Susy composedly. "You must go, now, Clarence. Quick! Remember what I said, — and don't breathe a word of this. Goodby."

But Clarence was standing still, breathless, hopelessly disturbed, and irresolute. Then he turned away mechanically towards the trail.

"Well, Clarence?"

She was looking at him half reproachfully, half coquettishly, with smiling, parted lips. He hastened to forget himself and his troubles upon them twice and thrice. Then she quickly disengaged herself, whispered, "Go, now," and, as Mary's call was repeated, Clarence heard her voice, high and clear, answering, "Here, dear," as he was plunging into the thicket.

He had scarcely reached the *madroño* tree again and remounted his horse, before he heard the sound of hoofs approaching from the road. In his present uneasiness he did not care to be discovered so near the rendezvous, and drew back into the shadow until the horseman should pass. It was Peyton, with a somewhat disturbed face, riding rapidly. Still less was he inclined to join or immediately follow him, but he was relieved when his host, instead of taking the direct road to the rancho, through the wild oats, turned off in the direction of the corral.

A moment later Clarence wheeled into the direct road, and presently found himself in the long afternoon shadows through the thickest of the grain. He was riding slowly, immersed in thought, when he was suddenly startled by a hissing noise at his ear, and what seemed to be the uncoiling stroke of a leaping serpent at his side. Instinctively he threw himself forward on his horse's neck, and as the animal shied into the grain, felt the crawling scrape and jerk of a horsehair lariat across his back and

down his horse's flanks. He reined in
indignantly and stood up in his stirrups.
Nothing was to be seen above the level of
the grain. Beneath him the trailing *riata*
had as noiselessly vanished as if it had been
indeed a gliding snake. Had he been the
victim of a practical joke, or of the blunder of some stupid vacquero? For he made
no doubt that it was the lasso of one of the
performers he had watched that afternoon.
But his preoccupied mind did not dwell long
upon it, and by the time he had reached the
wall of the old garden, the incident was forgotten.

CHAPTER VI.

RELIEVED of Clarence Brant's embarrass-
ing presence, Jim Hooker did not, however,
refuse to avail himself of that opportunity
to expound to the farmer and his family the
immense wealth, influence, and importance
of the friend who had just left him. Although Clarence's plan had suggested reticence, Hooker could not forego the pleasure
of informing them that "Clar" Brant had
just offered to let him into an extensive
land speculation. He had previously declined a large share or original location in a
mine of Clarence's, now worth a million,
because it was not "his style." But the
land speculation in a country of unsettled
titles and lawless men, he need not remind
them, required some experience of border
warfare. He would not say positively, although he left them to draw their own con-
clusions with gloomy significance, that this
was why Clarence had sought him. With
this dark suggestion, he took leave of Mr.

and Mrs. Hopkins and their daughter Phœbe the next day, not without some natural human emotion, and peacefully drove his team and wagon into the settlement of Fair Plains.

He was not prepared, however, for a sudden realization of his imaginative prospects. A few days after his arrival in Fair Plains, he received a letter from Clarence, explaining that he had not time to return to Hooker to consult him, but had, nevertheless, fulfilled his promise, by taking advantage of an opportunity of purchasing the Spanish "Sisters'" title to certain unoccupied lands near the settlement. As these lands in part joined the section already preëmpted and occupied by Hopkins, Clarence thought that Jim Hooker would choose that part for the sake of his neighbor's company. He inclosed a draft on San Francisco, for a sum sufficient to enable Jim to put up a cabin and "stock" the property, which he begged he would consider in the light of a loan, to be paid back in installments, only when the property could afford it. At the same time, if Jim was in difficulty, he was to inform him. The letter closed with a characteristic Clarence - like mingling of enthusiasm and older wisdom. "I wish you luck, Jim, but I see no reason why you should trust to it. I don't know of anything that could keep you from making yourself independent of any one, if you go to work with a *long aim* and don't fritter away your chances on short ones. If I were you, old fellow, I'd drop the Plains and the Indians out of my thoughts, or at least out of my *talk*, for a while; they won't help you in the long run. The people who believe you will be jealous of you; those who don't, will look down upon you, and if they get to questioning your little Indian romances, Jim, they'll be apt to question your civilized facts. That won't help you in the ranching .business, and that's your only real grip now." For the space of two or three hours after this, Jim was reasonably grateful and even subdued, — so much so that his employer, to whom he confided his good fortune, frankly confessed that he believed him from that unusual fact alone. Unfortunately, neither the practical lesson conveyed in this grim admission, nor the sentiment of gratitude, remained long with Jim. Another idea had taken possession of his fancy. Although the land nominated in his bill of sale had

been, except on the occasion of his own tem-
porary halt there, always unoccupied, un-
sought, and unclaimed, and although he was
amply protected .by legal certificates, he
gravely collected a posse of three or four
idlers from Fair Plains, armed them at his
own expense, and in the dead of night took
belligerent and forcible possession of the
peaceful domain which the weak generosity
and unheroic dollars of Clarence had purchased for him ! A martial camp-fire tem-
pered the chill night winds to the pulses of
the invaders, and enabled them to sleep on
their arms in the field they had won. The
morning sun revealed to the astonished
Hopkins family the embattled plain beyond,
with its armed sentries. Only then did Jim
Hooker condescend to explain the reason of
his warlike occupation, with dark hints of
the outlying "squatters" and "jumpers,"
whose incursions their boldness alone had
repulsed. The effect of this romantic situation upon the two women, with the slight
fascination of danger imported into their
quiet lives, may well be imagined. Possibly owing to some incautious questioning by
Mr. Hopkins, and some doubts of the discipline and sincerity of his posse, Jim dis-

charged them the next day; but during the erection of his cabin by some peaceful carpenters from the settlement, he returned to his gloomy preoccupation· and the ostentatious wearing of his revolvers. As an opulent and powerful neighbor, he took his meals with the family while his house was being built, and generally impressed them with a sense of security they had never missed.

Meantime, Clarence, duly informed of the installation of Jim as his tenant, underwent a severe trial. It was necessary for his plans that this should be kept a secret at present, and this was no easy thing for his habitually frank and open nature. He had once mentioned that he had met Jim at the settlement, but the information was received with such indifference by Susy, and such marked disfavor by Mrs. Peyton, that he said no more. He accompanied Peyton in his rides around the rancho, fully possessed himself of the details of its boundaries, the debatable lands held by the enemy, and listened with beating pulses, but a hushed tongue, to his host's ill-concealed misgivings.

"You see, Clarence, that lower terrace?"

he said, pointing to a far-reaching longitud-
inal plain beyond the corral; "it extends
from my corral to Fair Plains. That is
claimed by the sisters' title, and, as things
appear to be going, if a division of the land
is made it will be theirs. It's bad enough
to have this best grazing land lying just on
the flanks of the corral held by these rascals
at an absurd prohibitory price, but I am
afraid that it may be made to mean something even worse. According to the old
surveys, these terraces on different levels
were the natural divisions of the property,
— one heir or his tenant taking one, and
another taking another, — an easy distinc-
tion that saved the necessity of boundary
fencing or monuments, and gave no trouble
to people who were either kinsmen or lived
in lazy patriarchal concord. That is the
form of division they are trying to reëstab-
lish now. Well," he continued, suddenly
lifting his eyes to the young man's flushed
face, in some unconscious, sympathetic response to his earnest breathlessness, "although my boundary line extends half a
mile into that field, my house and garden
and corral *are actually upon that terrace or
level.*" They certainly appeared to Clarence

to be on the same line as the long field beyond. "If," went on Peyton, "such a decision
is made, these men will push on and claim
the house and everything on the terrace."

"But," said Clarence quickly, "you said
their title was only valuable where they
have got or can give *possession.* You already have yours. They can't take it from
you except by force."

"No," said Peyton grimly, "nor will
they dare to do it as long as I live to fight
them."

"But," persisted Clarence, with the same
singular hesitancy of manner, "why did n't
you purchase possession of at least that part
of the land which lies so dangerously near
your own house?"

"Because it was held by squatters, who
naturally preferred buying what might
prove a legal title to their land from these
impostors than to sell out their possession
to *me* at a fair price."

"But could n't you have bought from
them both?" continued Clarence.

"My dear Clarence, I am not a Crœsus
nor a fool. Only a man who was both
would attempt to treat with these rascals,
who would now, of course, insist that *their*

whole claim should be bought up at their own price by the man who was most concerned in defeating them."

He turned away a little impatiently. Fortunately he did not observe that Clarence's averted face was crimson with embarrassment, and that a faint smile hovered nervously about his mouth.

Since his late rendezvous with Susy, Clarence had had no chance to interrogate her further regarding her mysterious relative. That that shadowy presence was more or less exaggerated, if not an absolute myth, he more than half suspected, but of the discontent that had produced it, or the recklessness it might provoke, there was no doubt. She might be tempted to some act of folly. He wondered if Mary Rogers knew it. Yet, with his sensitive ideas of loyalty, he would have shrunk from any confidence with Mary regarding her friend's secrets, although he fancied that Mary's dark eyes sometimes dwelt upon him with mournful consciousness and premonition. He did not imagine the truth, that this romantic contemplation was only the result of Mary's conviction that Susy was utterly unworthy of his love. It so chanced one

morning that the vacquero who brought the
post from Santa Inez arrived earlier than
usual, and so anticipated the two girls, who
usually made a youthful point of meeting
him first as he passed the garden wall. The
letter bag was consequently delivered to
Mrs. Peyton in the presence of the others,
and a look of consternation passed between
the young girls. But Mary quickly seized
upon the bag as if with girlish and mischievous impatience, opened it, and glanced
within it.

"There are only three letters for you,"
she said, handing them to Clarence, with a
quick look of significance, which he failed to
comprehend, "and nothing for me or Susy."

"But," began the innocent Clarence, as
his first glance at the letters showed him
that one was directed to Susy, "here is " —

A wicked pinch on his arm that was
nearest Mary stopped his speech, and he
quickly put the letters in his pocket.

"Did n't you understand that Susy don't
want her mother to see that letter?" asked
Mary impatiently, when they were alone a
moment later.

"No," said Clarence simply, handing her
the missive.

Mary took it and turned it over in her hands.

"It 's in a man's handwriting," she said innocently.

"I had n't noticed it," returned Clarence with invincible naïveté, "but perhaps it is."

"And you hand it over for me to give to Susy, and ain't a bit curious to know who it 's from?"

"No," returned Clarence, opening his big eyes in smiling and apologetic wonder.

"Well," responded the young lady, with a long breath of melancholy astonishment, "certainly, of all things you are — you really *are!*" With which incoherency — apparently perfectly intelligible to herself — she left him. She had not herself the slightest idea who the letter was from; she only knew that Susy wanted it concealed.

The incident made little impression on Clarence, except as part of the general uneasiness he felt in regard to his old playmate. It seemed so odd to him that this worry should come from *her*, — that she herself should form the one discordant note in the Arcadian dream that he had found so sweet; in his previous imaginings it was the presence of Mrs. Peyton which he had

dreaded; she whose propinquity now seemed
so full of gentleness, reassurance, and repose. How worthy she seemed of any sac-
rifice he could make for her! He had seen
little of her for the last two or three days,
although her smile and greeting were always
ready for him. Poor Clarence did not
dream that she had found from certain in-
contestable signs and tokens, both in the
young ladies and himself, that he did not
require watching, and that becoming more
resigned to Susy's indifference, which
seemed so general and passive in quality,
she was no longer tortured by the sting of
jealousy.

Finding himself alone that afternoon, the
young man had wandered somewhat listlessly beyond the low adobe gateway. The
habits of the siesta obtained in a modified
form at the rancho. After luncheon, its
masters and employees usually retired, not
so much from the torrid heat of the afternoon sun, but from the first harrying of
the afternoon trades, whose monotonous
whistle swept round the walls. A straggling
passion vine near the gate beat and struggled against the wind. Clarence had stopped
near it, and was gazing with worried ab-

straction across the tossing fields, when a soft voice called his name.

It was a pleasant voice, — Mrs. Peyton's. He glanced back at the gateway; it was empty. He looked quickly to the right and left; no one was there.

The voice spoke again with the musical addition of a laugh; it seemed to come from the passion vine. Ah, yes; behind it, and half overgrown by its branches, was a long, narrow embrasured opening in the wall, defended by the usual Spanish grating, and still further back, as in the frame of a picture, the half length figure of Mrs. Peyton, very handsome and striking, too, with a painted picturesqueness from the effect of the checkered light and shade.

"You looked so tired and bored out there," she said. "I am afraid you are finding it very dull at the rancho. The prospect is certainly not very enlivening from where you stand."

Clarence protested with a visible pleasure in his eyes, as he held back a spray before the opening.

"If you are not afraid of being worse bored, come in here and talk with me. You have never seen this part of the house, I

think, — my own sitting-room. You reach
it from the hall in the gallery. But Lola
or Anita will show you the way."

He reëntered the gateway, and quickly
found the hall, — a narrow, arched passage,
whose black, tunnel-like shadows were abso-
lutely unaffected by the vivid, colorless
glare of the courtyard without, seen through
an opening at the end. The contrast was
sharp, blinding, and distinct; even the edges
of the opening were black; the outer light
halted on the threshold and never penetrated
within. The warm odor of verbena and
dried rose leaves stole from a half-open door
somewhere in the cloistered gloom. Guided
by it, Clarence presently found himself on
the threshold of a low-vaulted room. Two
other narrow embrasured windows like the
one he had just seen, and a fourth, wider
latticed casement, hung with gauze curtains,
suffused the apartment with a clear, yet
mysterious twilight that seemed its own.
The gloomy walls were warmed by bright-
fringed bookshelves, topped with trifles of
light feminine coloring and adornment.
Low easy-chairs and a lounge, small fanciful tables, a dainty desk, gayly colored
baskets of worsteds or mysterious kaleido-

scopic fragments, and vases of flowers pervaded the apartment with a mingled sense
of grace and comfort. There was a womanly refinement in its careless negligence,
and even the delicate wrapper of Japanese
silk, gathered at the waist and falling in
easy folds to the feet of the graceful mistress
of this charming disorder, looked a part of
its refined abandonment.

Clarence hesitated as on the threshold of
some sacred shrine. But Mrs. Peyton,
with her own hands, cleared a space for him
on the lounge.

"You will easily suspect from all this disorder, Mr. Brant, that I spend a greater
part of my time here, and that I seldom see
much company. Mr. Peyton occasionally
comes in long enough to stumble over a
footstool or upset a vase, and I think Mary
and Susy avoid it from a firm conviction
that there is work concealed in these baskets. But I have my books here, and in
the afternoons, behind these thick walls,
one forgets the incessant stir and restless-
ness of the dreadful winds outside. Just
now you were foolish enough to tempt them
while you were nervous, or worried, or listless. Take my word for it, it's a great

mistake. There is no more use fighting them, as I tell Mr. Peyton, than of fighting the people born under them. I have my own opinion that these winds were sent only to stir this lazy race of mongrels into activity, but they are enough to drive us Anglo-Saxons into nervous frenzy. Don't you think so? But you are young and energetic, and perhaps you are not affected by them."

She spoke pleasantly and playfully, yet with a certain nervous tension of voice and manner that seemed to illustrate her theory. At least, Clarence, in quick sympathy with her slightest emotion, was touched by it. There is no more insidious attraction in the persons we admire, than the belief that we know and understand their unhappiness, and that our admiration for them is lifted higher than a mere mutual instinctive sympathy with beauty or strength. This adorable woman had suffered. The very thought aroused his chivalry. It loosened, also, I fear, his quick, impulsive tongue.

Oh, yes; he knew it. He had lived under this whip of air and sky for three years, alone in a Spanish rancho, with only the native *peons* around him, and scarcely speaking his own tongue even to his guardian. He spent his mornings on horseback in fields like these, until the *vientos generales*, as they called them, sprang up and drove him nearly frantic; and his only relief was to bury himself among the books in his guardian's library, and shut out the world, — just as she did. The smile which hovered around the lady's mouth at that moment arrested Clarence, with a quick remembrance of their former relative positions, and a sudden conviction of his familiarity in suggesting an equality of experience, and he blushed. But Mrs. Peyton diverted his embarrassment with an air of interested absorption in his story, and said : —

"Then you know these people thoroughly, Mr. Brant? I am afraid that *we* do not."

Clarence had already gathered that fact within the last few days, and, with his usual impulsive directness, said so. A slight knitting of Mrs. Peyton's brows passed off, however, as he quickly and earnestly went on to say that it was impossible for the Peytons in their present relations to the natives to judge them, or to be judged by them fairly. How they were a childlike

race, credulous and trustful, but, like all
credulous and trustful people, given to re-
taliate when imposed upon with a larger
insincerity, exaggeration, and treachery.
How they had seen their houses and lands
occupied by strangers, their religion
scorned, their customs derided, their patriarchal society invaded by hollow civilization or frontier brutality — all this fortified
by incident and illustration, the outcome of
some youthful experience, and given with
the glowing enthusiasm of conviction.
Mrs. Peyton listened with the usual divided
feminine interest between subject and
speaker.

Where did this rough, sullen boy — as
she had known him — pick up this delicate
and swift perception, this reflective judgment, and this odd felicity of expression?
It was not possible that it was in him while
he was the companion of her husband's servants or the recognized "chum" of the
scamp Hooker. No. But if *he* could have
changed like this, why not Susy? Mrs.
Peyton, in the conservatism of her sex, had
never been quite free from fears of her
adopted daughter's hereditary instincts;
but, with this example before her, she now

took heart. Perhaps the change was coming slowly; perhaps even now what she thought was indifference and coldness was only some abnormal preparation or condition. But she only smiled and said: —

"Then, if you think those people have been wronged, you are not on our side, Mr. Brant?"

What to an older and more worldly man would have seemed, and probably was, only a playful reproach, struck Clarence deeply, and brought his pent-up feelings to his lips.

"*You* have never wronged them. You could n't do it; it is n't in your nature. I am on *your* side, and for you and yours always, Mrs. Peyton. From the first time I saw you on the plains, when I was brought, a ragged boy, before you by your husband, I think I would gladly have laid down my life for you. I don't mind telling you now that I was even jealous of poor Susy, so anxious was I for the smallest share in your thoughts, if only for a moment. You could have done anything with me you wished, and I should have been happy, — far happier than I have been ever since. I tell you this, Mrs. Peyton, now, because you have just doubted if I might be 'on your side,' but I have been longing to tell it all to you before, and it is that I am ready to do anything you want, — all you want, — to be on *your side* and *at your side*, now and forever."

He was so earnest and hearty, and above all so appallingly and blissfully happy, in this relief of his feelings, smiling as if it were the most natural thing in the world, and so absurdly unconscious of his twenty-two years, his little brown curling mustache, the fire in his wistful, yearning eyes, and, above all, of his clasped hands and lover-like attitude, that Mrs. Peyton — at first rigid as stone, then suffused to the eyes — cast a hasty glance round the apartment, put her handkerchief to her face, and laughed like a girl.

At which Clarence, by no means discomposed, but rather accepting her emotion as perfectly natural, joined her heartily, and added : —

"It's so, Mrs. Peyton; I'm glad I told you. You don't mind it, do you?"

But Mrs. Peyton had resumed her gravity, and perhaps a touch of her previous misgivings.

"I should certainly be very sorry," she

said, looking at him critically, "to object to your sharing your old friendship for your little playmate with her parents and guardians, or to your expressing it to *them* as frankly as to her."

She saw the quick change in his mobile face and the momentary arrest of its happy expression. She was frightened and yet puzzled. It was not the sensitiveness of a lover at the mention of the loved one's name, and yet it suggested an uneasy consciousness. If his previous impulsive outburst had been prompted honestly, or even artfully, by his passion for Susy, why had he looked so shocked when she spoke of her?

But Clarence, whose emotion had been caused by the sudden recall of his knowledge of Susy's own disloyalty to the woman whose searching eyes were upon him, in his revulsion against the deceit was, for an instant, upon the point of divulging all. Perhaps, if Mrs. Peyton had shown more confidence, he would have done so, and materially altered the evolution of this story. But, happily, it is upon these slight human weaknesses that your romancer depends, and Clarence, with no other reason than the instinctive sympathy of youth with youth in

its opposition to wisdom and experience, let
the opportunity pass, and took the responsibility of it out of the hands of this chroni-
cler.

Howbeit, to cover his confusion, he seized
upon the second idea that was in his mind,
and stammered, "Susy! Yes, I wanted to
speak to you about her." Mrs. Peyton
held her breath, but the young man went
on, although hesitatingly, with evident sincerity. "Have you heard from any of her
relations since — since — you adopted her?"

It seemed a natural enough question, although not the *sequitur* she had expected.
"No," she said carelessly. "It was well
understood, after the nearest relation — an
aunt by marriage — had signed her consent
to Susy's adoption, that there should be no
further intercourse with the family. There
seemed to us no necessity for reopening the
past, and Susy herself expressed no desire."
She stopped, and again fixing her handsome
eyes on Clarence, said, "Do you know any
of them?"

But Clarence by this time had recovered
himself, and was able to answer carelessly
and truthfully that he did not. Mrs. Peyton, still regarding him closely, added some-

what deliberately, "It matters little now what relations she has; Mr. Peyton and I have complete legal control over her until she is of age, and we can easily protect her from any folly of her own or others, or from any of the foolish fancies that sometimes overtake girls of her age and inexperience."

To her utter surprise, however, Clarence uttered a faint sigh of relief, and his face again recovered its expression of boyish happiness. "I'm glad of it, Mrs. Peyton," he said heartily. "No one could understand better what is for her interest in all things than yourself. Not," he said, with hasty and equally hearty loyalty to his old playmate, "that I think she would ever go against your wishes, or do anything that she knows to be wrong, but she is very young and innocent, — as much of a child as ever, don't you think so, Mrs. Peyton?"

It was amusing, yet nevertheless puzzling, to hear this boyish young man comment upon Susy's girlishness. And Clarence was serious, for he had quite forgotten in Mrs. Peyton's presence the impression of superiority which Susy had lately made upon him. But Mrs. Peyton returned to the charge, or, rather, to an attack upon what she conceived to be Clarence's old position.

"I suppose she does seem girlish compared to Mary Rogers, who is a much more reserved and quiet nature. But Mary is very charming, Mr. Brant, and I am really delighted to have her here with Susy. She has such lovely dark eyes and such good manners. She has been well brought up, and it is easy to see that her friends are superior people. I must write to them to thank them for her visit, and beg them to let her stay longer. I think you said you did n't know them? "

But Clarence, whose eyes had been thoughtfully and admiringly wandering over every characteristic detail of the charming apartment, here raised them to its handsome mistress, with an apologetic air and a "No" of such unaffected and complete abstraction, that she was again dumbfounded. Certainly, it could not be Mary in whom he was interested.

Abandoning any further inquisition for the present, she let the talk naturally fall upon the books scattered about the tables. The young man knew them all far better than she did, with a cognate knowledge of

others of which she had never heard. She
found herself in the attitude of receiving
information from this boy, whose boyish-
ness, however, seemed to have evaporated,
whose tone had changed with the subject,
and who now spoke with the conscious reserve of knowledge. Decidedly, she must
have grown rusty in her seclusion. This
came, she thought bitterly, of living alone;
of her husband's preoccupation with the
property; of Susy's frivolous caprices. At
the end of eight years to be outstripped by
a former cattle-boy of her husband's, and
to have her French corrected in a matter of
fact way by this recent pupil of the priests,
was really too bad! Perhaps he even
looked down upon Susy! She smiled dangerously but suavely.

"You must have worked *so* hard to edu-
cate yourself from nothing, Mr. Brant.
You couldn't read, I think, when you first
came to us. No? Could you really? I
know it has been very difficult for Susy to
get on with her studies in proportion. We
had so much to first eradicate in the way of
manners, style, and habits of thought which
the poor child had picked up from her companions, and for which *she* was not respon-

sible. Of course, with a boy that does not signify," she added, with feline gentleness.

But the barbed speech glanced from the young man's smoothly smiling abstraction.

"Ah, yes. But those were happy days, Mrs. Peyton," he answered, with an exasperating return of his previous boyish enthusiasm, "perhaps because of our ignorance. I don't think that Susy and I are any happier for knowing that the plains are not as flat as we believed they were, and that the sun doesn't have to burn a hole in them every night when it sets. But I know I believed that *you* knew everything. When I once saw you smiling over a book in your hand, I thought it must be a different one from any that I had ever seen, and perhaps made expressly for you. I can see you there still. Do you know," quite confidentially, "that you reminded me — of course *you* were much younger — of what I remembered of my mother?"

But Mrs. Peyton's reply of "Ah, indeed," albeit polite, indicated some coldness and lack of animation. Clarence rose quickly, but cast a long and lingering look around him.

"You will come again, Mr. Brant," said

the lady more graciously. "If you are going to ride now, perhaps you would try to meet Mr. Peyton. He is late already, and I am always uneasy when he is out alone, — particularly on one of those half-broken horses, which they consider good enough for riding here. *You* have ridden them before and understand them, but I am afraid that's another thing *we* have got to learn."

When the young man found himself again confronting the glittering light of the courtyard, he remembered the interview and the soft twilight of the boudoir only as part of a pleasant dream. There was a rude awakening in the fierce wind, which had increased with the lengthening shadows. It seemed to sweep away the half-sensuous comfort that had pervaded him, and made him coldly realize that he had done nothing to solve the difficulties of his relations to Susy. He had lost the one chance of confiding to Mrs. Peyton, — if he had ever really intended to do so. It was impossible for him to do it hereafter without a confession of prolonged deceit.

He reached the stables impatiently, where his attention was attracted by the sound of excited voices in the corral. Looking within, he was concerned to see that one of the vacqueros was holding the dragging bridle of a blown, dusty, and foam-covered horse, around whom a dozen idlers were gathered. Even beneath its coating of dust and foam and the half-displaced saddle blanket, Clarence immediately recognized the spirited *pinto* mustang which Peyton had ridden that morning.

"What's the matter?" said Clarence, from the gateway.

The men fell apart, glancing at each other. One said quickly in Spanish: —

"Say nothing to *him*. It is an affair of the house."

But this brought Clarence down like a bombshell among them, not to be overlooked in his equal command of their tongue and of them. "Ah! come, now. What drunken piggishness is this? Speak!"

"The *padron* has been — perhaps — thrown," stammered the first speaker. "His horse arrives, — but he does not. We go to inform the señora."

"No, you don't! mules and imbeciles! Do you want to frighten her to death? Mount, every one of you, and follow me!"

The men hesitated, but for only a moment. Clarence had a fine assortment of

Spanish epithets, expletives, and objurga-
tions, gathered in his *rodeo* experience at
El Refugio, and laid them about him with
such fervor and discrimination that two or
three mules, presumably with guilty con-
sciences, mistaking their direction, actually
cowered against the stockade of the corral
in fear. In another moment the vacqueros
had hastily mounted, and, with Clarence at
their head, were dashing down the road
towards Santa Inez. Here he spread them
in open order in the grain, on either side of
the track, himself taking the road.

They did not proceed very far. For
when they had reached the gradual slope
which marked the decline to the second terrace, Clarence, obeying an instinct as irre-
sistible as it was unaccountable, which for
the last few moments had been forcing itself
upon him, ordered a halt. The *casa* and
corral had already sunk in the plain behind them; it was the spot where the lasso
had been thrown at him a few evenings
before! Bidding the men converge slowly
towards the road, he went on more cautiously, with his eyes upon the track before
him. Presently he stopped. There was a
ragged displacement of the cracked and

crumbling soil and the unmistakable scoop
of kicking hoofs. As he stooped to examine
them, one of the men at the right uttered a
shout. By the same strange instinct Clarence knew that Peyton was found!

He was, indeed, lying there among the
wild oats at the right of the road, but without trace of life or scarcely human appearance. His clothes, where not torn and
shredded away, were partly turned inside
out; his shoulders, neck, and head were a
shapeless, undistinguishable mask of dried
earth and rags, like a mummy wrapping.
His left boot was gone. His large frame
seemed boneless, and, except for the cere-
ments of his mud-stiffened clothing, was
limp and sodden.

Clarence raised his head suddenly from a
quick examination of the body, and looked
at the men around him. One of them was
already cantering away. Clarence instantly
threw himself on his horse, and, putting
spurs to the animal, drew a revolver from
his holster and fired over the man's head.
The rider turned in his saddle, saw his pursuer, and pulled up.

"Go back," said Clarence, "or my next
shot won't *miss* you."

"I was only going to inform the señora," said the man with a shrug and a forced smile.

"*I* will do that," said Clarence grimly, driving him back with him into the waiting circle; then turning to them he said slowly, with deliberate, smileless irony, "And now, my brave gentlemen, — knights of the bull and gallant mustang hunters, — *I* want to inform *you* that I believe that Mr. Peyton was *murdered*, and if the man who killed him is anywhere this side of hell, *I* intend to find him. Good! You understand me! Now lift up the body, — you two, by the shoulders; you two, by the feet. Let your horses follow. For I intend that you four shall carry home your master in your arms, on foot. Now forward to the corral by the back trail. Disobey me, or step out of line and " — He raised the revolver ominously.

If the change wrought in the dead man before them was weird and terrifying, no less distinct and ominous was the change that, during the last few minutes, had come over the living speaker. For it was no longer the youthful Clarence who sat there, but a haggard, prematurely worn, desperate-looking avenger, lank of cheek, and injected of eye, whose white teeth glistened under the brown mustache and thin pale lips that parted when his restrained breath now and then hurriedly escaped them.

As the procession moved on, two men slunk behind with the horses.

"Mother of God! Who is this wolf's whelp?" said Manuel.

"Hush!" said his companion in a terrified whisper. "Have you not heard? It is the son of Hamilton Brant, the assassin, the duelist, — he who was fusiladed in Sonora." He made the sign of the cross quickly. "Jesus Maria! Let them look out who have cause, for the blood of his father is in him!"

CHAPTER VII.

WHAT other speech passed between Clarence and Peyton's retainers was not known, but not a word of the interview seemed to have been divulged by those present. It was generally believed and accepted that Judge Peyton met his death by being thrown from his half-broken mustang, and dragged at its heels, and medical opinion, hastily summoned from Santa Inez after the body had been borne to the corral, and stripped of its hideous encasings, declared that the neck had been broken, and death had followed instantaneously. An inquest was deemed unnecessary.

Clarence had selected Mary to break the news to Mrs. Peyton, and the frightened young girl was too much struck with the change still visible in his face, and the half authority of his manner, to decline, or even to fully appreciate the calamity that had befallen them. After the first benumbing shock, Mrs. Peyton passed into that strange

exaltation of excitement brought on by the
immediate necessity for action, followed by
a pallid calm, which the average spectator
too often unfairly accepts as incongruous,
inadequate, or artificial. There had also
occurred one of those strange compensations
that wait on Death or disrupture by catastrophe: such as the rude shaking down of
an unsettled life, the forcible realization of
what were vague speculations, the breaking
of old habits and traditions, and the unloos-
ing of half-conscious bonds. Mrs. Peyton,
without insensibility to her loss or disloyalty to her affections, nevertheless felt a relief to know that she was now really Susy's
guardian, free to order her new life wher-
ever and under what conditions she chose as
most favorable to it, and that she could dispose of this house that was wearying to her
when Susy was away, and which the girl
herself had always found insupportable.
She could settle this question of Clarence's
relations to her daughter out of hand without advice or opposition. She had a brother in the East, who would be summoned
to take care of the property. This consideration for the living pursued her, even
while the dead man's presence still awed

the hushed house; it was in her thoughts as she stood beside his bier and adjusted the flowers on his breast, which no longer moved for or against these vanities; and it stayed with her even in the solitude of her darkened room.

But if Mrs. Peyton was deficient, it was Susy who filled the popular idea of a mourner, and whose emotional attitude of a grief-stricken daughter left nothing to be desired. It was she who, when the house was filled with sympathizing friends from San Francisco and the few near neighbors who had hurried with condolences, was overflowing in her reminiscences of the ·dead man's goodness to her, and her own undying affection; who recalled ominous things that he had said, and strange premonitions of her own, the result of her ever-present filial anxiety; it was she who had hurried home that afternoon, impelled with vague fears of some impending calamity; it was she who drew a picture of Peyton as a doting and almost too indulgent parent, which Mary Rogers failed to recognize, and which brought back vividly to Clarence's recollection her own childish exaggerations of the Indian massacre. I am far from saying

that she was entirely insincere or merely
acting at these moments; at times she was
taken with a mild hysteria, brought on by
the exciting intrusion of this real event in
her monotonous life, by the attentions of
her friends, the importance of her suffering
as an only child, and the advancement of
her position as the heiress of the Robles
Rancho. If her tears were near the surface, they were at least genuine, and filmed
her violet eyes and reddened her pretty eye-
lids quite as effectually as if they had
welled from the depths of her being. Her
black frock lent a matured dignity to her
figure, and paled her delicate complexion
with the refinement of suffering. Even
Clarence was moved in that dark and haggard abstraction that had settled upon him
since his strange outbreak over the body of
his old friend.

The extent of that change had not been
noticed by Mrs. Peyton, who had only observed that Clarence had treated her grief
with a grave and silent respect. She was
grateful for that. A repetition of his boyish impulsiveness would have been distasteful to her at such a moment. She only
thought him more mature and more sub-

dued, and as the only man now in her household his services had been invaluable in the
emergency.

The funeral had taken place at Santa
Inez, where half the county gathered to pay
their last respects to their former fellow-
citizen and neighbor, whose legal and com-
bative victories they had admired, and whom
death had lifted into a public character.
The family were returning to the house the
same afternoon, Mrs. Peyton and the girls
in one carriage, the female house-servants
in another, and Clarence on horseback.
They had reached the first plateau, and
Clarence was riding a little in advance,
when an extraordinary figure, rising from
the grain beyond, began to gesticulate to him
wildly. Checking the driver of the first
carriage, Clarence bore down upon the
stranger. To his amazement it was Jim
Hooker. Mounted on a peaceful, unwieldy
plough horse, he was nevertheless accoutred
and armed after his most extravagant fashion. In addition to a heavy rifle across his
saddle-bow he was weighted down with a
knife and revolvers. Clarence was in no
mood for trifling, and almost rudely demanded his business.

"Gord, Clarence, it ain't foolin'. The Sisters' title was decided yesterday."

"I knew it, you fool! It's *your* title! You were already on your land and in possession. What the devil are you doing *here?*"

"Yes, — but," stammered Jim, "all the boys holding that title moved up here to 'make the division' and grab all they could. And I followed. And I found out that they were going to grab Judge Peyton's house, because it was on the line, if they could, and findin' you was all away, by Gord *they did!* and they're in it! And I stoled out and rode down here to warn ye."

He stopped, looked at Clarence, glanced darkly around him and then down on his accoutrements. Even in that supreme moment of sincerity, he could not resist the possibilities of the situation.

"It's as much as my life's worth," he said gloomily. "But," with a dark glance at his weapons, "I'll sell it dearly."

"Jim!" said Clarence, in a terrible voice, "you're not lying again?"

"No," said Jim hurriedly. "I swear it, Clarence! No! Honest Injin this time. And look. I'll help you. They ain't ex-

pectin' you yet, and they think ye 'll come
by the road. Ef I raised a scare off there
by the corral, while you 're creepin' *round
by the back*, mebbe you could get in while
they 're all lookin' for ye in front, don't
you see? I 'll raise a big row, and they
need n't know but what ye 've got wind of
it and brought a party with you from Santa
Inez."

In a flash Clarence had wrought a feasi-
ble plan out of Jim's fantasy.

"Good," he said, wringing his old companion's hand. "Go back quietly now;
hang round the corral, and when you see
the carriage climbing the last terrace raise
your alarm. Don't mind how loud it is,
there 'll be nobody but the servants in the
carriages."

He rode quickly back to the first carriage,
at whose window Mrs. Peyton's calm face
was already questioning him. He told her
briefly and concisely of the attack, and what
he proposed to do.

"You have shown yourself so strong in
matters of worse moment than this," he
added quietly, "that I have no fears for
your courage. I have only to ask you to
trust yourself to me, to put you back at once

in your own home. Your presence there, just now, is the one important thing, whatever happens afterwards."

She recognized his maturer tone and determined manner, and nodded assent. More than that, a faint fire came into her handsome eyes; the two girls kindled their own at that flaming beacon, and sat with flushed cheeks and suspended, indignant breath. They were Western Americans, and not over much used to imposition.

"You must get down before we raise the hill, and follow me on foot through the grain. I was thinking," he added, turning to Mrs. Peyton, "of your boudoir window."

She had been thinking of it, too, and nodded.

"The vine has loosened the bars," he said.

"If it hasn't, we must squeeze through them," she returned simply.

At the end of the terrace Clarence dismounted, and helped them from the carriage. He then gave directions to the coachmen to follow the road slowly to the corral in front of the *casa*, and tied his horse behind the second carriage. Then, with Mrs. Peyton and the two young girls, he plunged into the grain.

It was hot, it was dusty; their thin shoes slipped in the crumbling adobe, and the great blades caught in their crape draperies, but they uttered no complaint. Whatever ulterior thought was in their minds, they were bent only on one thing at that moment, — on entering the house at any hazard. Mrs. Peyton had lived long enough on the frontier to know the magic power of *possession*. Susy already was old enough to feel the acute feminine horror of the profanation of her own belongings by alien hands. Clarence, more cognizant of the whole truth than the others, was equally silent and determined; and Mary Rogers was fired with the zeal of loyalty.

Suddenly a series of blood-curdling yells broke from the direction of the corral, and they stopped. But Clarence at once recognized the well-known war-whoop imitation of Jim Hooker, — infinitely more gruesome and appalling than the genuine aboriginal challenge. A half dozen shots fired in quick succession had evidently the same friendly origin.

"Now is our time," said Clarence eagerly. "We must run for the house."

They had fortunately reached by this time

the angle of the adobe wall of the *casa*, and
the long afternoon shadows of the building
were in their favor. They pressed forward
eagerly with the sounds of Jim Hooker's
sham encounter still in their ears, mingled
with answering shouts of defiance from
strange voices within the building towards
the front.

They rapidly skirted the wall, even passing boldly before the back gateway, which
seemed empty and deserted, and the next
moment stood beside the narrow window of
the boudoir. Clarence's surmises were correct; the iron grating was not only loose,
but yielded to a vigorous wrench, the vine
itself acting as a lever to pull out the rusty
bars. The young man held out his hand,
but Mrs. Peyton, with the sudden agility of
a young girl, leaped into the window, followed by Mary and Susy. The inner casement yielded to her touch; the next moment
they were within the room. Then Mrs.
Peyton's flushed and triumphant face reappeared at the window.

"It's all right; the men are all in the
courtyard, or in the front of the house.
The boudoir door is strong, and we can bolt
them out."

"It won't be necessary," said Clarence quietly; "you will not be disturbed."

"But are you not coming in?" she asked timidly, holding the window open.

Clarence looked at her with his first faint smile since Peyton's death.

"Of course I am, but not in *that* way. I am going in by *the front gate.*"

She would have detained him, but, with a quick wave of his hand, he left her, and ran swiftly around the wall of the *casa* toward the front. The gate was half open; a dozen excited men were gathered before it and in the archway, and among them, whitened with dust, blackened with powder, and apparently glutted with rapine, and still holding a revolver in his hand, was Jim Hooker! As Clarence approached, the men quickly retreated inside the gate and closed it, but not before he had exchanged a meaning glance with Jim. When he reached the gate, a man from within roughly demanded his business.

"I wish to see the leader of this party," said Clarence quietly.

"I reckon you do," returned the man, with a short laugh. "But I kalkilate *he* don't return the compliment."

"He probably will when he reads this note to his employer," continued Clarence still coolly, selecting a paper from his pocketbook. It was addressed to Francisco Robles, Superintendent of the Sisters' Title, and directed him to give Mr. Clarence Brant free access to the property and the fullest information concerning it. The man took it, glanced at it, looked again at Clarence, and then passed the paper to a third man among the group in the courtyard. The latter read it, and approached the gate carelessly.

"Well, what do you want?"

"I am afraid you have the advantage of me in being able to transact business through bars," said Clarence, with slow but malevolent distinctness, "and as mine is important, I think you had better open the gate to me."

The slight laugh that his speech had evoked from the bystanders was checked as the leader retorted angrily: —

"That's all very well; but how do I know that you're the man represented in that letter? Pancho Robles may know you, but *I* don't."

"That you can find out very easily," said

Clarence. "There is a man among your party who knows me, — Mr. Hooker. Ask him."

The man turned, with a quick mingling of surprise and suspicion, to the gloomy, imperturbable Hooker. Clarence could not hear the reply of that young gentleman, but it was evidently not wanting in his usual dark, enigmatical exaggeration. The man surlily opened the gate.

"All the same," he said, still glancing suspiciously at Hooker, "I don't see what *he's* got to do with you."

"A great deal," said Clarence, entering the courtyard, and stepping into the veranda; "*he's one of my tenants.*"

"Your *what?*" said the man, with a coarse laugh of incredulity.

"My tenants," repeated Clarence, glancing around the courtyard carelessly. Nevertheless, he was relieved to notice that the three or four Mexicans of the party did not seem to be old retainers of the rancho. There was no evidence of the internal treachery he had feared.

"Your *tenants!*" echoed the man, with an uneasy glance at the faces of the others.

"Yes," said Clarence, with business brev-

ity; "and, for the matter of that, although
I have no reason to be particularly proud of
it, *so are you all.* You ask my business
here.   It seems to be the same as yours, —
to hold possession of this house!   With this
difference, however," he continued, taking
a document from his pocket.   "Here is the
certificate, signed by the County Clerk, of
the bill of sale of the entire Sisters' title
to *me.*   It includes the whole two leagues
from Fair Plains to the old boundary line
of this rancho, which you forcibly entered
this morning.   There is the document; examine it if you like.   The only shadow of
a claim you could have to this property you
would have to derive from *me.*   The only
excuse you could have for this act of lawlessness would be orders from *me.*   And all that
you have done this morning is only the assertion of *my* legal right to this house.   If
I disavow your act, as I might, I leave
you as helpless as any tramp that was ever
kicked from a doorstep, — as any burglar
that was ever collared on the fence by a
constable."

It was the truth.   There was no denying
the authority of the document, the facts of
the situation, or its ultimate power and sig-

nificance. There was consternation, stupe-
faction, and even a half-humorous recognition of the absurdity of their position on
most of the faces around him. Incongruous
as the scene was, it was made still more
grotesque by the attitude of Jim Hooker.
Ruthlessly abandoning the party of con-
victed trespassers, he stalked gloomily over
to the side of Clarence, with the air of having been all the time scornfully in the secret
and a mien of wearied victoriousness, and
thus halting, he disdainfully expectorated
tobacco juice on the ground between him
and his late companions, as if to form a line
of demarcation. The few Mexicans began
to edge towards the gateway. This defection
of his followers recalled the leader, who was
no coward, to himself again.

"Shut the gate, there!" he shouted.

As its two sides clashed together again,
he turned deliberately to Clarence.

"That's all very well, young man, as re-
gards the *title*. You may have *bought* up
the land, and legally own every square inch
of howling wilderness between this and San
Francisco, and I wish you joy of your d——d
fool's bargain; you may have got a whole
circus like that," pointing to the gloomy

Jim, "at your back. But with all your money and all your friends you've forgotten one thing. You have n't got possession, and we have."

"That's just where we differ," said Clarence coolly, "for if you take the trouble to examine the house, you will see that it is already in possession of Mrs. Peyton, — *my tenant.*"

He paused to give effect to his revelations. But he was, nevertheless, unprepared for an unrehearsed dramatic situation. Mrs. Peyton, who had been tired of waiting, and was listening in the passage, at the mention of her name, entered the gallery, followed by the young ladies. The slight look of surprise upon her face at the revelation she had just heard of Clarence's ownership, only gave the suggestion of her having been unexpectedly disturbed in her peaceful seclusion. One of the Mexicans turned pale, with a frightened glance at the passage, as if he expected the figure of the dead man to follow.

The group fell back. The game was over, — and lost. No one recognized it more quickly than the gamblers themselves. More than that, desperate and lawless as they were, they still retained the chivalry of Western men, and every hat was slowly doffed to the three black figures that stood silently in the gallery. And even apologetic speech began to loosen the clenched teeth of the discomfited leader.

"We — were — told there was no one in the house," he stammered.

"And it was the truth," said a pert, youthful, yet slightly affected voice. "For we climbed into the window just as you came in at the gate."

It was Susy's words that stung their ears again; but it was Susy's pretty figure, suddenly advanced and in a slightly theatrical attitude, that checked their anger. There had been a sudden ominous silence, as the whole plot of rescue seemed to be revealed to them in those audacious words. But a sense of the ludicrous, which too often was the only perception that ever mitigated the passions of such assemblies, here suddenly asserted itself. The leader burst into a loud laugh, which was echoed by the others, and, with waving hats, the whole party swept peacefully out through the gate.

"But what does all this mean about *your* purchasing the land, Mr. Brant?" said Mrs.

Peyton quickly, fixing her eyes intently on Clarence.

A faint color — the useless protest of his truthful blood — came to his cheek.

"The hcuse is *yours*, and yours alone, Mrs. Peyton. The purchase of the sisters' title was a private arrangement between Mr. Peyton and myself, in view of an emergency like this."

She did not, however, take her proud, searching eyes from his face, and he was forced to turn away.

"It was *so* like dear, good, thoughtful papa," said Susy. "Why, bless me," in a lower voice, "if that isn't that lying old Jim Hooker standing there by the gate!"

CHAPTER VIII.

JUDGE PEYTON had bequeathed his entire property unconditionally to his wife. But his affairs were found to be greatly in disorder, and his papers in confusion, and although Mrs. Peyton could discover no actual record of the late transaction with Mr. Brant, which had saved her the possession of the homestead, it was evident that he had spent large sums in speculative attempts to maintain the integrity of his estate. That enormous domain, although perfectly unencumbered, had been nevertheless unremunerative, partly through the costs of litigation and partly through the systematic depredations to which its great size and long line of unprotected boundary had subjected it. It had been invaded by squatters and "jumpers," who had sown and reaped crops without discovery; its cattle and wild horses had strayed or been driven beyond its ill-defined and hopeless limits. Against these difficulties the widow felt herself unable and unwilling to contend, and with the advice of her friends and her lawyer, she concluded to sell the estate, except that portion covered by the Sisters' title, which, with the homestead, had been reconveyed to her by Clarence. She retired with Susy to the house in San Francisco, leaving Clarence to occupy and hold the *casa*, with her servants, for her until order was restored. The Robles Rancho thus became the headquarters of the new owner of the Sisters' title, from which he administered its affairs, visited its incumbencies, overlooked and surveyed its lands, and — occasionally — collected its rents. There were not wanting critics who averred that these were scarcely remunerative, and that the young San Francisco fine gentleman, who was only Hamilton Brant's son, after all, yet who wished to ape the dignity and degree of a large landholder, had made a very foolish bargain. I grieve to say that one of his own tenants, namely, Jim Hooker, in his secret heart inclined to that belief, and looked upon Clarence's speculation as an act of far-seeing and inordinate vanity.

Indeed, the belligerent Jim had partly — and of course darkly — intimated some-

thing of this to Susy in their brief reunion
at the *casa* during the few days that followed its successful reoccupation. And
Clarence, remembering her older caprices,
and her remark on her first recognition of
him, was quite surprised at the easy familiarity of her reception of this forgotten companion of their childhood. But he was still
more concerned in noticing, for the first
time, a singular sympathetic understanding of each other, and an odd similarity of
occasional action and expression between
them. It was a part of this monstrous pe-
culiarity that neither the sympathy nor the
likeness suggested any particular friendship
or amity in the pair, but rather a mutual
antagonism and suspicion. Mrs. Peyton,
coldly polite to Clarence's former *companion,* but condescendingly gracious to his
present *tenant* and retainer, did not notice
it, preoccupied with the annoyance and pain
of Susy's frequent references to the old days
of their democratic equality.

"You don't remember, Jim, the time
that you painted my face in the wagon, and
got me up as an Indian papoose?" she said
mischievously.

But Jim, who had no desire to recall his

previous humble position before Mrs. Peyton or Clarence, was only vaguely responsive. Clarence, although joyfully touched at this seeming evidence of Susy's loyalty to the past, nevertheless found himself even more acutely pained at the distress it caused Mrs. Peyton, and was as relieved as she was by Hooker's reticence. For he had seen little of Susy since Peyton's death, and there had been no repetition of their secret interviews. Neither had he, nor she as far as he could judge, noticed the omission. He had been more than usually kind, gentle, and protecting in his manner towards her, with little reference, however, to any response from her, yet he was vaguely conscious of some change in his feelings. He attributed it, when he thought of it at all, to the exciting experiences through which he had passed; to some sentiment of responsibility to his dead friend; and to another secret preoccupation that was always in his mind. He believed it would pass in time. Yet he felt a certain satisfaction that she was no longer able to trouble him, except, of course, when she pained Mrs. Peyton, and then he was half conscious of taking the old attitude of the dead husband in mediating between them. Yet so great was his inexperience that he believed, with pathetic simplicity of perception, that all this was due to the slow maturing of his love for her, and that he was still able to make her happy. But this was something to be thought of later. Just now Providence seemed to have offered him a vocation and a purpose that his idle adolescence had never known. He did not dream that his capacity for patience was only the slow wasting of his love.

Meantime that more wonderful change and recreation of the Californian landscape, so familiar, yet always so young, had come to the rancho. The league-long terrace that had yellowed, whitened, and wasted for half a year beneath a staring, monotonous sky, now under sailing clouds, flying and broken shafts of light, and sharply defined lines of rain, had taken a faint hue of resurrection. The dust that had muffled the roads and byways, and choked the low oaks that fringed the sunken *cañada*, had long since been laid. The warm, moist breath of the southwest trades had softened the hard, dry lines of the landscape, and restored its color as of a picture over which a damp sponge had

been passed. The broad expanse of plateau
before the *casa* glistened and grew dark.
The hidden woods of the *cañada*, cleared
and strengthened in their solitude, dripped
along the trails and hollows that were now
transformed into running streams. The
distinguishing *madroño* near the entrance
to the rancho had changed its crimson summer suit and masqueraded in buff and
green.

Yet there were leaden days, when half the
prospect seemed to be seen through palisades
of rain; when the slight incline between the
terraces became a tumultuous cascade, and
the surest hoofs slipped on trails of unctu-
ous mud; when cattle were bogged a few
yards from the highway, and the crossing of
the turnpike road was a dangerous ford.
There were days of gale and tempest, when
the shriveled stalks of giant oats were
stricken like trees, and lay across each other
in rigid angles, and a roar as of the sea came
up from the writhing treetops in the sunken
valley. There were long weary nights of
steady downpour, hammering on the red tiles
of the *casa*, and drumming on the shingles
of the new veranda, which was more terrible to be borne. Alone, but for the ser-

vants, and an occasional storm-stayed tenant from Fair Plains, Clarence might have, at such times, questioned the effect of this seclusion upon his impassioned nature. But he had already been accustomed to monastic seclusion in his boyish life at El Refugio, and he did not reflect that, for that very reason, its indulgences might have been dangerous. From time to time letters reached him from the outer world of San Francisco, — a few pleasant lines from Mrs. Peyton, in answer to his own chronicle of his half stewardship, giving the news of the family, and briefly recounting their movements. She was afraid that Susy's sensitive nature chafed under the restriction of mourning in the gay city, but she trusted to bring her back for a change to Robles when the rains were over. This was a poor substitute for those brief, happy glimpses of the home circle which had so charmed him, but he accepted it stoically. He wandered over the old house, from which the perfume of domesticity seemed to have evaporated, yet, notwithstanding Mrs. Peyton's playful permission, he never intruded upon the sanctity of the boudoir, and kept it jealously locked.

He was sitting in Peyton's business room

one morning, when Incarnacion entered.
Clarence had taken a fancy to this Indian,
half steward, half vacquero, who had recip-
rocated it with a certain dog-like fidelity,
but also a feline indirectness that was part
of his nature. He had been early prepossessed with Clarence through a kinsman at
El Refugio, where the young American's
generosity had left a romantic record among
the common people. He had been pleased
to approve of his follies before the knowledge of his profitless and lordly land purchase had commended itself to him as cor-
roborative testimony. "Of true hidalgo
blood, mark you," he had said oracularly.
"Wherefore was his father sacrificed by
mongrels! As to the others, believe me, —
bah!"

He stood there, sombrero in hand, murky
and confidential, steaming through his soaked
serape and exhaling a blended odor of equine
perspiration and cigarette smoke.

"It was, perhaps, as the master had
noticed, a brigand's own day! Bullying,
treacherous, and wicked! It blew you off
your horse if you so much as lifted your
arms and let the wind get inside your *serape ;*
and as for the mud, — caramba! in fifty

varas your forelegs were like bears, and your hoofs were earthen plasters!"

Clarence knew that Incarnacion had not sought him with mere meteorological information, and patiently awaited further developments. The vacquero went on: —

"But one of the things this beast of a weather did was to wash down the stalks of the grain, and to clear out the trough and hollows between, and to make level the fields, and — look you! to uncover the stones and rubbish and whatever the summer dust had buried. Indeed, it was even as a miracle that José Mendez one day, after the first showers, came upon a silver button from his *calzas*, which he had lost in the early summer. And it was only that morning that, remembering how much and with what fire Don Clarencio had sought the missing boot from the foot of the Señor Peyton when his body was found, he, Incarnacion, had thought he would look for it on the *falda* of the second terrace. And behold, Mother of God! it was there! Soaked with mud and rain, but the same as when the señor was alive. To the very spur!"

He drew the boot from beneath his *serape* and laid it before Clarence. The young

man instantly recognized it, in spite of its
weather-beaten condition and its air of grotesque and drunken inconsistency to the
usually trim and correct appearance of Peyton when alive. "It is the same," he said,
in a low voice.

"Good!" said Incarnacion. "Now, if
Don Clarencio will examine the American
spur, he will see — what? A few horse-
hairs twisted and caught in the sharp points
of the rowel. Good! Is it the hair of the
horse that Señor rode? Clearly not; and
in truth not. It is too long for the flanks
and belly of the horse; it is not the same
color as the tail and the mane. How comes
it there? It comes from the twisted horse-
hair rope of a *riata*, and not from the
braided cowhide thongs of the regular lasso
of a vacquero. The lasso slips not much,
but holds; the *riata* slips much and stran-
gles."

"But Mr. Peyton was not strangled,"
said Clarence quickly.

"No, for the noose of the *riata* was perhaps large, — who knows? It might have
slipped down his arms, pinioned him, and
pulled him off. Truly! — such has been
known before. Then on the ground it

slipped again, or he perhaps worked it off to his feet where it caught on his spur, and then he was dragged until the boot came off, and behold! he was dead."

This had been Clarence's own theory of the murder, but he had only half confided it to Incarnacion. He silently examined the spur with the accusing horse-hair, and placed it in his desk. Incarnacion continued: —

"There is not a vacquero in the whole rancho who has a horse-hair *riata*. We use the braided cowhide; it is heavier and stronger; it is for the bull and not the man. The horse-hair *riata* comes from over the range — south."

There was a dead silence, broken only by the drumming of the rain upon the roof of the veranda. Incarnacion slightly shrugged his shoulders.

"Don Clarencio does not know the southern county? Francisco Robles, cousin of the 'Sisters,' — he they call 'Pancho,' — comes from the south. Surely when Don Clarencio bought the title he saw Francisco, for he was the steward?"

"I dealt only with the actual owners and through my bankers in San Francisco," returned Clarence abstractedly.

Incarnacion looked through the yellow
corners of his murky eyes at his master.

"Pedro Valdez, who was sent away by
Señor Peyton, is the foster-brother of Francisco. They were much together. Now
that Francisco is rich from the gold Don
Clarencio paid for the title, they come not
much together. But Pedro is rich, too.
Mother of God! He gambles and is a fine
gentleman. He holds his head high, — even
over the Americanos he gambles with.
Truly, they say he can shoot with the best
of them. He boasts and swells himself,
this Pedro! He says if all the old families
were like him, they would drive those western swine back over the mountains again."

Clarence raised his eyes, caught a subtle
yellow flash from Incarnacion's, gazed at
him suddenly, and rose.

"I don't think I have ever seen him," he
said quietly. "Thank you for bringing me
the spur. But keep the knowledge of it to
yourself, good Nascio, for the present."

Nascio nevertheless still lingered. Per-
ceiving which, Clarence handed him a cigarette and proceeded to light one himself.
He knew that the vacquero would reroll his,
and that that always deliberate occupation

would cover and be an excuse for further confidence.

"The Señora Peyton does not perhaps meet this Pedro in the society of San Francisco?"

"Surely not. The señora is in mourning and goes not out in society, nor would she probably go anywhere where she would meet a dismissed servant of her husband."

Incarnacion slowly lit his cigarette, and said between the puffs, "And the señorita — she would not meet him?"

"Assuredly not."

"And," continued Incarnacion, throwing down the match and putting his foot on it, "if this boaster, this turkey-cock, says she did, you could put him out like that?"

"Certainly," said Clarence, with an easy confidence he was, however, far from feeling, "if he really *said* it — which I doubt."

"Ah, truly," said Incarnacion; "who knows? It may be another Señorita Silsbee."

"The señora's adopted daughter is called *Miss Peyton*, friend Nascio. You forget yourself," said Clarence quietly.

"Ah, pardon!" said Incarnacion with effusive apology; "but she was born Silsbee.

Everybody knows it; she herself has told it
to Pepita. The Señor Peyton bequeathed
his estate to the Señora Peyton. He named
not the señorita! Eh, what would you? It
is the common cackle of the barnyard. But
I say 'Mees Silsbee.' For look you. There
is a Silsbee of Sacramento, the daughter of
her aunt, who writes letters to her. Pepita
has seen them! And possibly it is only that
Mees of whom the brigand Pedro boasts."

"Possibly," said Clarence, "but as far as
this rancho is concerned, friend Nascio, thou
wilt understand — and I look to thee to
make the others understand — that there is
no Señorita *Silsbee* here, only the Señorita *Peyton*, the respected daughter of the
señora thy mistress!" He spoke with the
quaint mingling of familiarity and paternal
gravity of the Spanish master — a faculty
he had acquired at El Refugio in a like
vicarious position, and which never failed
as a sign of authority. "And now," he
added gravely, "get out of this, friend, with
God's blessing, and see that thou remem-
berest what I told thee."

The retainer, with equal gravity, stepped
backwards, saluted with his sombrero until
the stiff brim scraped the floor, and then
solemnly withdrew.

Left to himself, Clarence remained for an instant silent and thoughtful before the oven-like hearth. So! everybody knew Susy's real relations to the Peytons, and everybody but Mrs. Peyton, perhaps, knew that she was secretly corresponding with some one of her own family. In other circumstances he might have found some excuse for this assertion of her independence and love of her kindred, but in her attitude towards Mrs. Peyton it seemed monstrous. It appeared impossible that Mrs. Peyton should not have heard of it, or suspected the young girl's disaffection. Perhaps she had, — it was another burden laid upon her shoulders, — but the proud woman had kept it to herself. A film of moisture came across his eyes. I fear he thought less of the suggestion of Susy's secret meeting with Pedro, or Incarnacion's implied suspicions that Pedro was concerned in Peyton's death, than of this sentimental possibility. He knew that Pedro had been hated by the others on account of his position; he knew the instinctive jealousies of the race and their predisposition to extravagant misconstruction. From what he had gathered, and particularly from the voices he had over-

heard on the Fair Plains Road, it seemed to
him that Pedro was more capable of merce-
nary intrigue than physical revenge. He
was not aware of the irrevocable affront put
upon Pedro by Peyton, and he had consequently attached no importance to Peyton's
own half - scornful intimation of the only
kind of retaliation that Pedro would be
likely to take. The unsuccessful attempt
upon himself he had always thought might
have been an accident, or if it was really a
premeditated assault, it might have been intended actually for *himself* and not Peyton,
as he had first thought, and his old friend
had suffered for *him*, through some mistake
of the assailant. The purpose, which alone
seemed wanting, might have been to remove
Clarence as a possible witness who had overheard their conspiracy — how much of it
they did not know — on the Fair Plains
Road that night. The only clue he held to
the murderer in the spur locked in his desk,
merely led him beyond the confines of the
rancho, but definitely nowhere else. It was,
however, some relief to know that the crime
was not committed by one of Peyton's retainers, nor the outcome of domestic treachery.

After some consideration he resolved to
seek Jim Hooker, who might be possessed
of some information respecting Susy's relations, either from the young girl's own confidences or from Jim's personal knowledge
of the old frontier families. From a sense
of loyalty to Susy and Mrs. Peyton, he had
never alluded to the subject before him, but
since the young girl's own indiscretion had
made it a matter of common report, however
distasteful it was to his own feelings, he felt
he could not plead the sense of delicacy for
her. He had great hopes in what he had
always believed was only her exaggeration
of fact as well as feeling. And he had an
instinctive reliance on her fellow *poseur's*
ability to detect it. A few days later, when
he found he could safely leave the rancho
alone, he rode to Fair Plains.

The floods were out along the turnpike
road, and even seemed to have increased
since his last journey. The face of the landscape had changed again. One of the lower
terraces had become a wild mere of sedge
and reeds. The dry and dusty bed of a forgotten brook had reappeared, a full-banked
river, crossing the turnpike and compelling
a long détour before the traveler could ford

it. But as he approached the Hopkins farm and the opposite clearing and cabin of Jim Hooker, he was quite unprepared for a still more remarkable transformation. The cabin, a three-roomed structure, and its cattle-shed had entirely disappeared! There were no traces or signs of inundation. The land lay on a gentle acclivity above the farm and secure from the effects of the flood, and a part of the ploughed and cleared land around the site of the cabin showed no evidence of overflow on its black, upturned soil. But the house was gone! Only a few timbers too heavy to be removed, the blighting erasions of a few months of occupation, and the dull, blackened area of the site itself were to be seen. The fence alone was intact.

Clarence halted before it, perplexed and astonished. Scarcely two weeks had elapsed since he had last visited it and sat beneath its roof with Jim, and already its few ruins had taken upon themselves the look of years of abandonment and decay. The wild land seemed to have thrown off its yoke of cultivation in a night, and nature rioted again with all its primal forces over the freed soil. Wild oats and mustard were springing already in the broken furrows, and lank vines were slimily spreading over a few scattered but still unseasoned and sappy shingles. Some battered tin cans and fragments of old clothing looked as remote as if they had been relics of the earliest immigration.

Clarence turned inquiringly towards the Hopkins farmhouse across the road. His arrival, however, had already been noticed, as the door of the kitchen opened in an anticipatory fashion, and he could see the slight figure of Phœbe Hopkins in the doorway, backed by the overlooking heads and shoulders of her parents. The face of the young girl was pale and drawn with anxiety, at which Clarence's simple astonishment took a shade of concern.

"I am looking for Mr. Hooker," he said uneasily. "And I don't seem to be able to find either him or his house."

"And you don't know what's gone of him?" said the girl quickly.

"No; I have n't seen him for two weeks."

"There, I told you so!" said the girl, turning nervously to her parents. "I knew it. He has n't seen him for two weeks." Then, looking almost tearfully at Clarence's face, she said, "No more have we."

"But," said Clarence impatiently, "something must have happened. Where is his house?"

"Taken away by them jumpers," interrupted the old farmer; "a lot of roughs that pulled it down and carted it off in a jiffy before our very eyes without answerin' a civil question to me or her. But he wasn't there, nor before, nor since."

"No," added the old woman, with flashing eyes, "or he'd let 'em have what ther' was in his six-shooters."

"No, he wouldn't, mother," said the girl impatiently, "he'd *changed*, and was agin all them ideas of force and riotin'. He was for peace and law all the time. Why, the day before we missed him he was tellin' me California never would be decent until people obeyed the laws and the titles were settled. And for that reason, because he wouldn't fight agin the law, or without the consent of the law, they've killed him, or kidnapped him away."

The girl's lips quivered, and her small brown hands twisted the edges of her blue checked apron. Although this new picture of Jim's peacefulness was as astounding and unsatisfactory as his own disappearance, there was no doubt of the sincerity of poor Phœbe's impression.

In vain did Clarence point out to them there must be some mistake; that the trespassers — the so-called jumpers — really belonged to the same party as Hooker, and would have no reason to dispossess him; that, in fact, they were all *his*, Clarence's, tenants. In vain he assured them of Hooker's perfect security in possession; that he could have driven the intruders away by the simple exhibition of his lease, or that he could have even called a constable from the town of Fair Plains to protect him from mere lawlessness. In vain did he assure them of his intention to find his missing friend, and reinstate him at any cost. The conviction that the unfortunate young man had been foully dealt with was fixed in the minds of the two women. For a moment Clarence himself was staggered by it.

"You see," said the young girl, with a kindling face, "the day before he came back from Robles, ther' were some queer men hangin' round his cabin, but as they were the same kind that went off with him the day the Sisters' title was confirmed, we thought nothing of it. But when he came

back from you he seemed worried and anxious, and was n't a bit like himself. We
thought perhaps he 'd got into some trouble
there, or been disappointed. He had n't,
had he, Mr. Brant?" continued Phœbe,
with an appealing look.

"By no means," said Clarence warmly.
"On the contrary, he was able to do his
friends good service there, and was successful in what he attempted. Mrs. Peyton
was very grateful. Of course he told you
what had happened, and what he did for
us," continued Clarence, with a smile.

He had already amused himself on the
way with a fanciful conception of the exaggerated account Jim had given of his ex-
ploits. But the bewildered girl shook her
head.

"No, he did n't tell us *anything.*"

Clarence was really alarmed. This un-
precedented abstention of Hooker's was portentous.

"He did n't say anything but what I told
you about law and order," she went on;
"but that same night we heard a good deal
of talking and shouting in the cabin and
around it. And the next day he was talking with father, and wanting to know how

he kept his land without trouble from out-siders."

"And I said," broke in Hopkins, "that I guessed folks did n't bother a man with women folks around, and that I kalkilated that *I* was n't quite as notorious for fightin' as he was."

"And he said," also interrupted Mrs. Hopkins, "and quite in his nat'ral way, too, — gloomy like, you remember, Cyrus," appealingly to her husband, — "that that was his curse."

The smile that flickered around Clarence's mouth faded, however, as he caught sight of Phœbe's pleading, interrogating eyes. It was really too bad. Whatever change had come over the rascal it was too evident that his previous belligerent personality had had its full effect upon the simple girl, and that, hereafter, one pair of honest eyes would be wistfully following him.

Perplexed and indignant, Clarence again closely questioned her as to the personnel of the trespassing party who had been seen once or twice since passing over the field. He had at last elicited enough information to identify one of them as Gilroy, the leader of the party that had invaded Robles

Rancho. His cheek flushed. Even if they had wished to take a theatrical and momentary revenge on Hooker for the passing treachery to them which they had just discovered, although such retaliation was only transitory, and they could not hold the land, it was an insult to Clarence himself, whose tenant Jim was, and subversive of all their legally acquired rights. He would confront this Gilroy at once; his half-wild encampment was only a few miles away, just over the boundaries of the Robles estate. Without stating his intention, he took leave of the Hopkins family with the cheerful assurance that he would probably return with some news of Hooker, and rode away.

The trail became more indistinct and unfrequented as it diverged from the main road, and presently lost itself in the slope towards the east. The horizon grew larger: there were faint bluish lines upon it which he knew were distant mountains; beyond this a still fainter white line — the Sierran snows. Presently he intersected a trail running south, and remarked that it crossed the highway behind him, where he had once met the two mysterious horsemen. They had evidently reached the terrace through

the wild oats by that trail. A little farther on were a few groups of sheds and canvas tents in a bare and open space, with
scattered cattle and horsemen, exactly like
an encampment, or the gathering of a country fair. As Clarence rode down towards
them he could see that his approach was
instantly observed, and that a simultaneous
movement was made as if to anticipate him.
For the first time he realized the possible
consequences of his visit, single-handed, but
it was too late to retrace his steps. With
a glance at his holster, he rode boldly forward to the nearest shed. A dozen men
hovered near him, but something in his
quiet, determined manner held them aloof.
Gilroy was on the threshold in his shirt-
sleeves. A single look showed him that
Clarence was alone, and with a careless gesture of his hand he warned away his own
followers.

"You 've got a sort of easy way of drop-
pin' in whar you ain't invited, Brant," he
said with a grim smile, which was not, however, without a certain air of approval.
"Got it from your father, did n't you?"

"I don't know, but I don't believe *he*
ever thought it necessary to warn twenty

men of the approach of one," replied Clarence, in the same tone. "I had no time to stand on ceremony, for I have just come from Hooker's quarter section at Fair Plains."

Gilroy smiled again, and gazed abstractedly at the sky.

"You know as well as I do," said Clarence, controlling his voice with an effort, "that what you have done there will have to be undone, if you wish to hold even those lawless men of yours together, or keep yourself and them from being run into the brush like highwaymen. I 've no fear for that. Neither do I care to know what was your motive in doing it; but I can only tell you that if it was retaliation, I alone was and still am responsible for Hooker's action at the rancho. I came here to know just what you have done with him, and, if necessary, to take his place."

"You 're just a little too previous in your talk, I reckon, Brant," returned Gilroy lazily, "and as to legality, I reckon we stand on the same level with yourself, just here. Beginnin' with what you came for: as we don't know where your Jim Hooker is, and as we ain't done anythin' to *him*, we don't exackly see what we could do with *you* in his place. Ez to our motives, — well, we've got a good deal to say about *that*. We reckoned that he wasn't exackly the kind of man we wanted for a neighbor. His pow'ful fightin' style didn't suit us peaceful folks, and we thought it rather worked agin this new 'law and order' racket to have such a man about, to say nuthin' of it prejudicin' quiet settlers. He had too many revolvers for one man to keep his eye on, and was altogether too much steeped in blood, so to speak, for ordinary washin' and domestic purposes! His hull get up was too deathlike and clammy; so we persuaded him to leave. We just went there, all of us, and exhorted him. We stayed round there two days and nights, takin' turns, talkin' with him, nuthin' more, only selecting subjects in his own style to please him, until he left! And then, as we didn't see any use for his house there, we took it away. Them's the cold facts, Brant," he added, with a certain convincing indifference that left no room for doubt, "and you can stand by 'em. Now, workin' back to the first principle you laid down, — that we'll have to *undo* what **we 've** *done*, — we don't agree with you,

for we 've taken a leaf outer your own book.
We 've got it here in black and white.
We 've got a bill o' sale of Hooker's house
and possession, and we 're on the land in
place of him, — *as your tenants.*" He re-
entered the shanty, took a piece of paper
from a soap-box on the shelf, and held it
out to Clarence. "Here it is. It 's a fair
and square deal, Brant. We gave him, as
it says here, a hundred dollars for it! No
humbuggin', but the hard cash, by Jiminy!
And he took the money."

The ring of truth in the man's voice was
as unmistakable as the signature in Jim's
own hand. Hooker had sold out! Clarence
turned hastily away.

"We don't know where he went," continued Gilroy grimly, "but I reckon you ain't
over anxious to see him *now*. And I kin
tell ye something to ease your mind, — he
did n't require much persuadin'. And I
kin tell ye another, if ye ain't above takin'
advice from folks that don't pertend to give
it," he added, with the same curious look of
interest in his face. "You 've done well to
get shut of him, and if you got shut of a
few more of his kind that you trust to,
you 'd do better."

As if to avoid noticing any angry reply from the young man, he reëntered the cabin and shut the door behind him. Clarence felt the uselessness of further parley, and rode away.

But Gilroy's Parthian arrow rankled as he rode. He was not greatly shocked at Jim's defection, for he was always fully conscious of his vanity and weakness; but he was by no means certain that Jim's extravagance and braggadocio, which he had found only amusing and, perhaps, even pathetic, might not be as provocative and prejudicial to others as Gilroy had said. But, like all sympathetic and unselfish natures, he sought to find some excuse for his old companion's weakness in his own mistaken judgment. He had no business to bring poor Jim on the land, to subject his singular temperament to the temptations of such a life and such surroundings; he should never have made use of his services at the rancho. He had done him harm rather than good in his ill-advised, and, perhaps, *selfish* attempts to help him. I have said that Gilroy's parting warning rankled in his breast, but not ignobly. It wounded the surface of his sensitive nature, but could not taint or corrupt the pure, wholesome blood of the gentleman beneath it. For in Gilroy's warning he saw only his own shortcomings. A strange fatality had marked his friendships. He had been no help to Jim; he had brought no happiness to Susy or Mrs. Peyton, whose disagreement his visit seemed to have accented. Thinking over the mysterious attack upon himself, it now seemed to him possible that, in some obscure way, his presence at the rancho had precipitated the more serious attack on Peyton. If, as it had been said, there was some curse upon his inheritance from his father, he seemed to have made others share it with him. He was riding onward abstractedly, with his head sunk on his breast and his eyes fixed upon some vague point between his horse's sensitive ears, when a sudden, intelligent, forward pricking of them startled him, and an apparition arose from the plain before him that seemed to sweep all other sense away.

It was the figure of a handsome young horseman as abstracted as himself, but evidently on better terms with his own personality. He was dark haired, sallow cheeked, and blue eyed, — the type of the old Spanish Californian. A burnt-out cigarette was in his mouth, and he was riding a roan mustang with the lazy grace of his race. But what arrested Clarence's attention more than his picturesque person was the narrow, flexible, long coil of gray horse-hair *riata* which hung from his saddle-bow, but whose knotted and silver-beaded terminating lash he was swirling idly in his narrow brown hand. Clarence knew and instantly recognized it as the ordinary fanciful appendage of a gentleman rider, used for tethering his horse on lonely plains, and always made the object of the most lavish expenditure of decoration and artistic skill. But he was as suddenly filled with a blind, unreasoning sense of repulsion and fury, and lifted his eyes to the man as he approached. What the stranger saw in Clarence's blazing eyes no one but himself knew, for his own became fixed and staring; his sallow cheeks grew lanker and livid; his careless, jaunty bearing stiffened into rigidity, and swerving his horse to one side he suddenly passed Clarence at a furious gallop. The young American wheeled quickly, and for an instant his knees convulsively gripped the flanks of his horse to follow. But the

next moment he recalled himself, and with
an effort began to collect his thoughts.
What was he intending to do, and for what
reason! He had met hundreds of such
horsemen before, and caparisoned and accoutred like this, even to the *riata*. And
he certainly was not dressed like either of
the mysterious horsemen whom he had overheard that moonlight evening. He looked
back; the stranger had already slackened
his pace, and was slowly disappearing.
Clarence turned and rode on his way.

CHAPTER IX.

WITHOUT disclosing the full extent of Jim's defection and desertion, Clarence was able to truthfully assure the Hopkins family of his personal safety, and to promise that he would continue his quest, and send them further news of the absentee. He believed it would be found that Jim had been called away on some important business, but that not daring to leave his new shanty exposed and temptingly unprotected, he had made a virtue of necessity by selling it to his neighbors, intending to build a better house on its site after his return. Having comforted Phœbe, and impulsively conceived further plans for restoring Jim to her, — happily without any recurrence of his previous doubts as to his own efficacy as a special Providence, — he returned to the rancho. If he thought again of Jim's defection and Gilroy's warning, it was only to strengthen himself to a clearer perception of his unselfish duty and singleness of purpose. He

would give up brooding, apply himself more
practically to the management of the property, carry out his plans for the foundation
of a Landlords' Protective League for the
southern counties, become a candidate for
the Legislature, and, in brief, try to fill
Peyton's place in the county as he had at
the rancho. He would endeavor to become
better acquainted with the half-breed labor-
ers on the estate and avoid the friction between them and the Americans; he was conscious that he had not made that use of his
early familiarity with their ways and lan-
guage which he might have done. If, occasionally, the figure of the young Spaniard
whom he had met on the lonely road ob-
truded itself on him, it was always with the
instinctive premonition that he would meet
him again, and the mystery of the sudden
repulsion be in some way explained. Thus
Clarence! But the momentary impulse that
had driven him to Fair Plains, the eagerness to set his mind at rest regarding Susy
and her relatives, he had utterly forgotten.

Howbeit some of the energy and enthusiasm that he breathed into these various
essays made their impression. He succeeded
in forming the Landlords' League; under a

commission suggested by him the straggling boundaries of Robles and the adjacent claims were resurveyed, defined, and mutually protected; even the lawless Gilroy, from extending an amused toleration to the young administrator, grew to recognize and accept him; the *peons* and vacqueros began to have faith in a man who acknowledged them sufficiently to rebuild the ruined Mission Chapel on the estate, and save them the long pilgrimage to Santa Inez on Sundays and saints' days; the San Francisco priest imported from Clarence's old college at San José, and an habitual guest at Clarence's hospitable board, was grateful enough to fill his flock with loyalty to the young *padron*.

He had returned from a long drive one afternoon, and had just thrown himself into an easy-chair with the comfortable consciousness of a rest fairly earned. The dull embers of a fire occasionally glowed in the oven-like hearth, although the open casement of a window let in the soft breath of the southwest trades. The angelus had just rung from the restored chapel, and, mellowed by distance, seemed to Clarence to lend that repose to the wind-swept landscape that it had always lacked.

Suddenly his quick ear detected the sound
of wheels in the ruts of the carriage way.
Usually his visitors to the *casa* came on
horseback, and carts and wagons used only
the lower road.   As the sound approached
nearer, an odd fancy filled his heart with
unaccountable pleasure.   Could it be Mrs.
Peyton making an unexpected visit to the
rancho?   He held his breath.   The vehicle
was now rolling on into the *patio*.   The
clatter of hoofs and a halt were followed by
the accents of women's voices.   One seemed
familiar.   He rose quickly, as light footsteps ran along the corridor, and then the
door opened impetuously to the laughing
face of Susy!

He came towards her hastily, yet with
only the simple impulse of astonishment.
He had no thought of kissing her, but as he
approached, she threw her charming head
archly to one side, with a mischievous knitting of her brows and a significant gesture
towards the passage, that indicated the
proximity of a stranger and the possibility
of interruption.

"Hush!   Mrs. McClosky's here," she
whispered.

"Mrs. McClosky?" repeated Clarence
vaguely.

"Yes, of course," impatiently. "My Aunt Jane. Silly! We just cut away down here to surprise you. Aunty's never seen the place, and here was a good chance."

"And your mother — Mrs. Peyton? Has she — does she?" — stammered Clarence.

"Has she — does she?" mimicked Susy, with increasing impatience. "Why, of course she *does n't* know anything about it. She thinks I'm visiting Mary Rogers at Oakland. And I am — *afterwards*," she laughed. "I just wrote to Aunt Jane to meet me at Alameda, and we took the stage to Santa Inez and drove on here in a buggy. Was n't it real fun? Tell me, Clarence! You don't say anything! Tell me — was n't it real fun?"

This was all so like her old, childlike, charming, irresponsible self, that Clarence, troubled and bewildered as he was, took her hands and drew her like a child towards him.

"Of course," she went on, yet stopping to smell a rosebud in his buttonhole, "I have a perfect right to come to my own home, goodness knows! and if I bring my own aunt, a married woman, with me, — although," loftily, "there may be a young

unmarried gentleman alone there, — still I
fail to see any impropriety in it!'"

He was still holding her; but in that instant her manner had completely changed
again; the old Susy seemed to have slipped
away and evaded him, and he was retaining
only a conscious actress in his arms.

"Release me, Mr. Brant, please," she
said, with a languid affected glance behind
her; "we are not alone."

Then, as the rustling of a skirt sounded
nearer in the passage, she seemed to change
back to her old self once more, and with a
lightning flash of significance whispered, —

"She knows everything!"

To add to Clarence's confusion, the woman who entered cast a quick glance of
playful meaning on the separating youthful
pair. She was an ineffective blonde with a
certain beauty that seemed to be gradually
succumbing to the ravages of paint and powder rather than years; her dress appeared
to have suffered from an equally unwise
excess of ornamentation and trimming, and
she gave the general impression of having
been intended for exhibition in almost any
other light than the one in which she happened to be. There were two or three mud-

stains on the laces of her sleeve and under-
skirt that were obtrusively incongruous.
Her voice, which had, however, a ring of
honest intention in it, was somewhat over-
strained, and evidently had not yet adjusted
itself to the low-ceilinged, conventual-like
building.

"There, children, don't mind me! I
know I'm not on in this scene, but I got
nervous waiting there, in what you call the
'sallon,' with only those Greaser servants
staring round me in a circle, like a regular
chorus. My! but it's anteek here — regular anteek — Spanish." Then, with a glance
at Clarence, "So this is Clarence Brant,
— your Clarence? Interduce me, Susy."

In his confusion of indignation, pain, and
even a certain conception of the grim ludi-
crousness of the situation, Clarence grasped
despairingly at the single sentence of Susy's.
"In my own home." Surely, at least, it
was *her own home*, and as he was only the
business agent of her adopted mother, he
had no right to dictate to her under what
circumstances she should return to it, or
whom she should introduce there. In her
independence and caprice Susy might easily
have gone elsewhere with this astounding

relative, and would Mrs. Peyton like it
better? Clinging to this idea, his instinct
of hospitality asserted itself. He welcomed
Mrs. McClosky with nervous effusion: —

"I am only Mrs. Peyton's major domo·
here, but any guest of her *daughter's* is
welcome."

"Yes," said Mrs. McClosky, with ostentatious archness, "I reckon Susy and I understand your position here, and you 've got
a good berth of it. But we won't trouble
you much on Mrs. Peyton's account, will
we, Susy? And now she and me will just
take a look around the shanty, — it is real
old Spanish anteek, ain't it? — and sorter
take stock of it, and you young folks will
have to tear yourselves apart for a while,
and play propriety before me. You 've got
to be on your good behavior while I 'm here,
I can tell you! I 'm a heavy old 'doo-anna.'
Ain't I, Susy? School-ma'ms and mother
superiors ain't in the game with *me* for discipline."

She threw her arms around the young
girl's waist and drew her towards her affec-
tionately, an action that slightly precipitated
some powder upon the black dress of her
niece. Susy glanced mischievously at Clar-

ence, but withdrew her eyes presently to let
them rest with unmistakable appreciation
and admiration on her relative. · A pang
shot through Clarence's breast. He had
never seen her look in that way at Mrs.
Peyton. Yet here was this stranger, provincial, overdressed, and extravagant, whose
vulgarity was only made tolerable through
her good humor, who had awakened that
interest which the refined Mrs. Peyton had
never yet been able to touch. As Mrs.
McClosky swept out of the room with Susy
he turned away with a sinking heart.

Yet it was necessary that the Spanish
house servants should not suspect this trea-
son to their mistress, and Clarence stopped
their childish curiosity about the stranger
with a careless and easy acceptance of Susy's
sudden visit in the light of an ordinary oc-
currence, and with a familiarity towards
Mrs. McClosky which became the more distasteful to him in proportion as he saw that
it was evidently agreeable to her. But,
easily responsive, she became speedily confidential. Without a single question from
himself, or a contributing remark from Susy,
in half an hour she had told him her whole
history. How, as Jane Silsbee, an elder

sister of Susy's mother, she had early eloped from the paternal home in Kansas with McClosky, a strolling actor. How she had married him and gone on the stage under his stage name, effectively preventing any recognition by her family. How, coming to California, where her husband had become manager of the theatre at Sacramento, she was indignant to find that her only surviving relation, a sister-in-law, living in the same place, had for a money consideration given up all claim to the orphaned Susy, and how she had resolved to find out "if the poor child was happy." How she succeeded in finding out that she was not happy. How she wrote to her, and even met her secretly at San Francisco and Oakland, and how she had undertaken this journey partly for "a· lark," and partly to see Clarence and the property. There was no doubt of the speaker's sincerity; with this outrageous candor there was an equal obliviousness of any indelicacy in her conduct towards Mrs. Peyton that seemed hopeless. Yet he must talk plainly to her; he must say to her what he could not say to Susy; upon *her* Mrs. Peyton's happiness — he believed he was thinking of Susy's also — depended. He must take the first opportunity of speaking to her alone.

That opportunity .came sooner than he had expected. After dinner, Mrs. Mc-Closky turned to Susy, and playfully telling her that she had "to talk business" with Mr. Brant, bade her go to the salon and await her. When the young girl left the room, she looked at Clarence, and, with that assumption of curtness with which coarse but kindly natures believe they overcome the difficulty of delicate subjects, said abruptly: —

"Well, young man, now what's all this between you and Susy? I'm looking after her interests — same as if she was my own girl. If you've got anything to say, now's your time. And don't you shilly-shally too long over it, either, for you might as well know that a girl like that can have her pick and choice, and be beholden to no one; and when she don't care to choose, there's me and my husband ready to do for her all the same. We mightn't be able to do the anteek Spanish Squire, but we've got our own line of business, and it's a comfortable one."

To have this said to him under the roof

of Mrs. Peyton, from whom, in his sensitiveness, he had thus far jealously guarded his own secret, was even more than Clarence's gentleness could stand, and fixed his wavering resolution.

"I don't think we quite understand each other, Mrs. McClosky," he said coldly, but with glittering eyes. "I have certainly something to say to you; if it is not on a subject as pleasant as the one you propose, it is, nevertheless, one that I think you and I are more competent to discuss together."

Then, with quiet but unrelenting directness, he pointed out to her that Susy was a legally adopted daughter of Mrs. Peyton, and, as a minor, utterly under her control; that Mrs. Peyton had no knowledge of any opposing relatives; and that Susy had not only concealed the fact from her, but that he was satisfied that Mrs. Peyton did not even know of Susy's discontent and alienation; that she had tenderly and carefully brought up the helpless orphan as her own child, and even if she had not gained her affection was at least entitled to her obedience and respect; that while Susy's girlish caprice and inexperience excused *her* conduct, Mrs. Peyton and her friends would

have a right to expect more consideration
from a person of Mrs. McClosky's maturer
judgment. That for these reasons, and as
the friend of Mrs. Peyton, whom he could
alone recognize as Susy's guardian and the
arbiter of her affections, he must decline to
discuss the young girl with any reference to
himself or his own intentions.

An unmistakable flush asserted itself
under the lady's powder.

"Suit yourself, young man, suit yourself,"
she said, with equally direct resentment and
antagonism; "only mebbee you 'll let me
tell you that Jim McClosky ain't no fool,
and mebbee knows what lawyers think of
an arrangement with a sister-in-law that
leaves a real sister out! Mebbee that 's a
'Sister's title' you ain't thought of, Mr.
Brant! And mebbee you 'll find out that
your chance o' gettin' Mrs. Peyton's consent ain't as safe to gamble on as you
reckon it is. And mebbee, what 's more
to the purpose, if you *did* get it, it might
not be just the trump card to fetch Susy
with! And to wind up, Mr. Brant, when
you *do* have to come down to the bed-rock
and me and Jim McClosky, you may find
out that him and me have discovered a bet-

ter match for Susy than the son of old Ham
Brant, who is trying to play the Spanish
grandee off his father's money on a couple
of women.   And we may n't have to go far
to do it — or to get *the real thing*, Mr.
Brant!"

Too heartsick and disgusted to even
notice the slur upon himself or the import
of her last words, Clarence only rose and
bowed as she jumped up from the table.
But as she reached the door he said, half
appealingly: —

"Whatever are your other intentions,
Mrs. McClosky, as we are both Susy's
guests, I beg you will say nothing of this
to her while we are here, and particularly
that you will not allow her to think for a
moment that I have discussed *my* relations
to her with anybody."

She flung herself out of the door without
a reply; but on entering the dark low-ceilinged drawing-room she was surprised to
find that Susy was not there.   She was consequently obliged to return to the veranda,
where Clarence had withdrawn, and to somewhat ostentatiously demand of the servants
that Susy should be sent to her room at
once.   But the young girl was not in her

own room, and was apparently nowhere to
be found. Clarence, who had now fully
determined as a last resource to make a direct appeal to Susy herself, listened to this
fruitless search with some concern. She
could not have gone out in the rain, which
was again falling. She might be hiding
somewhere to avoid a recurrence of the
scene she had perhaps partly overheard.
He turned into the corridor that led to Mrs.
Peyton's boudoir. As he knew that it was
locked, he was surprised to see by the dim
light of the hanging lamp that a duplicate
key to the one in his desk was in the lock.
It must be Susy's, and the young girl had
probably taken refuge there. He knocked
gently. There was a rustle in the room
and the sound of a chair being moved, but
no reply. Impelled by a sudden instinct
he opened the door, and was met by a cool
current of air from some open window. At
the same moment the figure of Susy approached him from the semi-darkness of the
interior.

"I did not know you were here," said
Clarence, much relieved, he knew not why,
"but I am glad, for I wanted to speak with
you alone for a few moments."

She did not reply, but he drew a match from his pocket and lit the two candles which he knew stood on the table. The wick of one was still warm, as if it had been recently extinguished. As the light slowly radiated, he could see that she was regarding him with an air of affected unconcern, but a somewhat heightened color. It was like her, and not inconsistent with his idea that she had come there to avoid an after scene with Mrs. McClosky or himself, or perhaps both. The room was not disarranged in any way. The window that was opened was the casement of the deep embrasured one in the rear wall, and the light curtain before it still swayed occasionally in the night wind.

"I 'm afraid I had a row with your aunt, Susy," he began lightly, in his old familiar way; "but I had to tell her I did n't think her conduct to Mrs. Peyton was exactly the square thing towards one who had been as devoted to you as she has been."

"Oh, for goodness' sake, don't go over all that again," said Susy impatiently. "I 've had enough of it."

Clarence flushed, but recovered himself.

"Then you overheard what I said, and know what I think," he said calmly.

"I knew it *before*," said the young girl, with a slight supercilious toss of the head, and yet a certain abstraction of manner as she went to the window and closed it. "Anybody could see it! I know you always wanted me to stay here with Mrs. Peyton, and be coddled and monitored and catechised and shut up away from any one, until *you* had been coddled and monitored and catechised by somebody else sufficiently to suit her ideas of your being a fit husband for me. I told aunty it was no use our coming here to — to " —

"To do what?" asked Clarence.

"To put some spirit into you," said the young girl, turning upon him sharply; "to keep you from being tied to that woman's apron-strings. To keep her from making a slave of you as she would of me. But it is of no use. Mary Rogers was right when she said you had no wish to please anybody but Mrs. Peyton, and no eyes for anybody but her. And if it had n't been too ridiculous, considering her age and yours, she 'd say you were dead in love with her."

For an instant Clarence felt the blood

rush to his face and then sink away, leaving
him pale and cold. The room, which had
seemed to whirl around him, and then fade
away, returned with appalling distinctness,
— the distinctness of memory, — and a vision
of the first day that he had seen Mrs. Peyton sitting there, as he seemed to see her
now. For the first time there flashed upon
him the conviction that the young girl had
spoken the truth, and had brusquely brushed
the veil from his foolish eyes. He *was* in
love with Mrs. Peyton! That was what his
doubts and hesitation regarding Susy meant.
That alone was the source, secret, and limit
of his vague ambition.

But with the conviction came a singular
calm. In the last few moments he seemed
to have grown older, to have loosed the
bonds of. old companionship with Susy, and
the later impression she had given him of
her mature knowledge, and moved on far
beyond her years and experience. And it
was with an authority that was half paternal,
and in a voice he himself scarcely recognized, that he said: —

"If I did not know you were prejudiced
by a foolish and indiscreet woman, I should
believe that you were trying to insult me as

you have your adopted mother, and would save you the pain of doing both in *her* house by leaving it now and forever. But because I believe you are controlled against your best instinct by that woman, I shall remain here with you to frustrate her as best I can, or until I am able to lay everything before Mrs. Peyton except the foolish speech you have just made."

The young girl laughed. "Why not *that* one too, while you're about it? See what she'll say."

"I shall tell her," continued Clarence calmly, "only what *you* yourself have made it necessary for me to tell her to save you from folly and disgrace, and only enough to spare her the mortification of hearing it first from her own servants."

"Hearing *what* from her own servants? What do you mean? How dare you?" demanded the young girl sharply.

She was quite real in her anxiety now, although her attitude of virtuous indignation struck him as being like all her emotional expression, namely, acting.

"I mean that the servants know of your correspondence with Mrs. McClosky, and that she claims to be your aunt," returned

Clarence. "They know that you confided to Pepita. They believe that either Mrs. McClosky or you have seen " —

He had stopped suddenly. He was about to say that the servants (particularly Incarnacion) knew that Pedro had boasted of having met Susy, when, for the first time, the tremendous significance of what he had hitherto considered as merely an idle falsehood flashed upon him.

"Seen whom?" repeated Susy in a higher voice, impatiently stamping her foot.

Clarence looked at her, and in her excited, questioning face saw a confirmation of his still half - formed suspicions. In his own abrupt pause and knitted eyebrows she must have read his thoughts also. Their eyes met. Her violet pupils dilated, trembled, and then quickly shifted as she suddenly stiffened into an attitude of scornful indifference, almost grotesque in its unreality. His eyes slowly turned to the window, the door, the candles on the table and the chair before it, and then came back to her face again. Then he drew a deep breath.

"I give no heed to the idle gossip of servants, Susy," he said slowly. "I have no belief that you have ever contemplated anything worse than an act of girlish folly, or the gratification of a passing caprice. Neither do I want to appeal to you or frighten you, but I must tell you now, that I know certain facts that might make such a simple act of folly monstrous, inconceivable in *you*, and almost accessory to a crime! I can tell you no more. But so satisfied am I of such a possibility, that I shall not scruple to take any means — the strongest — to prevent even the remotest chance of it. Your aunt has been looking for you; you had better go to her now. I will close the room and lock the door. Meantime, I should advise you not to sit so near an open window with a candle at night in this locality. Even if it might not be dangerous for you, it might be fatal to the foolish creatures it might attract."

He took the key from the door as he held it open for her to pass out. She uttered a shrill little laugh, like a nervous, mischievous child, and, slipping out of her previous artificial attitude as if it had been a mantle, ran out of the room.

CHAPTER X.

As Susy's footsteps died away, Clarence
closed the door, walked to the window, and
examined it closely. The bars had been
restored since he had wrenched them off to
give ingress to the family on the day of
recapture. He glanced around the room;
nothing seemed to have been disturbed.
Nevertheless he was uneasy. The suspicions of a frank, trustful nature when once
aroused are apt to be more general and far-
reaching than the specific distrusts of the
disingenuous, for they imply the overthrow
of a whole principle and not a mere detail.
Clarence's conviction that Susy had seen
Pedro recently since his dismissal led him
into the wildest surmises of her motives. It
was possible that without her having reason
to suspect Pedro's greater crime, he might
have confided to her his intention of reclaim-
ing the property and installing her as the
mistress and chatelaine of the rancho. The
idea was one that might have appealed to

Susy's theatrical imagination. He recalled
Mrs. McClosky's sneer at his own preten-
sions and her vague threats of a rival of
more lineal descent. The possible infidelity
of Susy to himself touched him lightly
when the first surprise was over; indeed, it
scarcely could be called infidelity, if she
knew and believed Mary Rogers's discovery;
and the conviction that he and she had
really never loved each other now enabled
him, as he believed, to look at her conduct
dispassionately. Yet it was her treachery
to Mrs. Peyton and not to himself that
impressed him most, and perhaps made him
equally unjust, through his affections.

He extinguished the candles, partly from
some vague precautions he could not explain,
and partly to think over his fears in the
abstraction and obscurity of the semi-darkness. The higher windows suffused a faint
light on the ceiling, and, assisted by the
dark lantern-like glow cast on the opposite
wall by the tunnel of the embrasured window, the familiar outlines of the room and
its furniture came back to him. Somewhat
in this fashion also, in the obscurity and
quiet, came back to him the events he had
overlooked and forgotten. He recalled now

some gossip of the servants, and hints dropped by Susy of a violent quarrel between Peyton and Pedro, which resulted in Pedro's dismissal, but which now seemed clearly attributable to some graver cause than inattention and insolence. He recalled Mary Rogers's playful pleasantries with Susy about Pedro, and Susy's mysterious air, which he had hitherto regarded only as part of her exaggeration. He remembered Mrs. Peyton's unwarrantable uneasiness about Susy, which he had either overlooked or referred entirely to himself; she must have suspected something. To his quickened imagination, in this ruin of his faith and trust, he believed that Hooker's defection was either part of the conspiracy, or that he had run away to avoid being implicated with Susy in its discovery. This, too, was the significance of Gilroy's parting warning. He and Mrs. Peyton alone had been blind and confiding in the midst of this treachery, and even *he* had been blind to his own real affections.

The wind had risen again, and the faint light on the opposite wall grew tremulous and shifting with the movement of the foliage without. But presently the glow became quite obliterated, as if by the intervention of some opaque body outside the window. He rose hurriedly and went to the casement. But at the same moment he fancied he heard the jamming of a door or window in quite another direction, and his examination of the casement before him showed him only the silver light of the thinly clouded sky falling uninterruptedly through the bars and foliage on the interior of the whitewashed embrasure. Then a conception of his mistake flashed across him. The line of the *casa* was long, straggling, and exposed elsewhere; why should the attempt to enter or communicate with any one within be confined only to this single point? And why not satisfy himself at once if any trespassers were lounging around the walls, and then confront them boldly in the open? Their discovery and identification was as important as the defeat of their intentions.

He relit the candle, and, placing it on a small table by the wall beyond the visual range of the window, rearranged the curtain so that, while it permitted the light to pass out, it left the room in shadow. He then opened the door softly, locked it behind him, and passed noiselessly into the hall. Susy's

and Mrs. McClosky's rooms were at the
further end of the passage, but between them
and the boudoir was the open *patio*, and the
low murmur of the voices of servants, who
still lingered until he should dismiss them
for the night. Turning back, he moved
silently down the passage, until he reached
the narrow arched door to the garden. This
he unlocked and opened with the same
stealthy caution. The rain had recom-
menced. Not daring to risk a return to his
room, he took from a peg in the recess an
old waterproof cloak and "sou'wester" of
Peyton's, which still hung there, and passed
out into the night, locking the door behind
him. To keep the knowledge of his secret
patrol from the stablemen, he did not attempt to take out his own horse, but trusted
to find some vacquero's mustang in the corral. By good luck an old "Blue Grass"
hack of Peyton's, nearest the stockade as
he entered, allowed itself to be quickly
caught. Using its rope headstall for a
bridle, Clarence vaulted on its bare back,
and paced cautiously out into the road.
Here he kept the curve of the long-line of
stockade until he reached the outlying field
where, half hidden in the withered, sapless,

but still standing stalks of grain, he slowly
began a circuit of the *casa*.

The misty gray dome above him, which
an invisible moon seemed to have quicksil-
vered over, alternately lightened and darkened with passing gusts of fine rain. Nevertheless he could see the outline of the
broad quadrangle of the house quite distinctly, except on the west side, where a
fringe of writhing willows beat the brown
adobe walls with their imploring arms at
every gust. Elsewhere nothing moved; the
view was uninterrupted to where the shining,
watery sky met the equally shining, watery
plain. He had already made a half circuit
of the house, and was still noiselessly pick-
ing his way along the furrows, muffled with
soaked and broken - down blades, and the
velvety upspringing of the "volunteer"
growth, when suddenly, not fifty yards before him, without sound or warning, a figure
rode out of the grain upon the open cross-
road, and deliberately halted with a listless,
abstracted, waiting air. Clarence instantly
recognized one of his own vacqueros, an
undersized half-breed, but he as instantly
divined that he was only an outpost or confederate, stationed to give the alarm. The

same precaution had prevented each hearing the other, and the lesser height of the vac-quero had rendered him indistinguishable as he preceded Clarence among the grain. As the young man made no doubt that the real trespasser was nearer the *casa*, along the line of willows, he wheeled to intercept him without alarming his sentry. Unfortunately, his horse answered the rope bridle clumsily, and splashed in striking out. The watcher quickly raised his head, and Clarence knew that his only chance was now to suppress him. Determined to do this at any hazard, with a threatening gesture he charged boldly down upon him.

But he had not crossed half the distance between them when the man uttered an appalling cry, so wild and despairing that it seemed to chill even the hot blood in Clarence's veins, and dashed frenziedly down the cross-road into the interminable plain. Before Clarence could determine if that cry was a signal or an involuntary outburst, it was followed instantly by the sound of frightened and struggling hoofs clattering against the wall of the *casa*, and a swaying of the shrubbery near the back gate of the *patio*. Here was his real quarry! Without hesitation he dug his heels into the flanks of his horse and rode furiously towards it. As he approached, a long tremor seemed to pass through the shrubbery, with the retreating sound of horse hoofs. The unseen trespasser had evidently taken the alarm and was fleeing, and Clarence dashed in pursuit. Following the sound, for the shrubbery hid the fugitive from view, he passed the last wall of the *casa;* but it soon became evident that the unknown had the better horse. The hoof-beats grew fainter and fainter, and at times appeared even to cease, until his own approach started them again, eventually to fade away in the distance. In vain Clarence dug his heels into the flanks of his heavier steed, and regretted his own mustang; and when at last he reached the edge of the thicket he had lost both sight and sound of the fugitive. The descent to the lower terrace lay before him empty and desolate. The man had escaped!

He turned slowly back with baffled anger and vindictiveness. However, he had prevented something, although he knew not what. The principal had got away, but he had identified his confederate, and for the first time held a clue to his mysterious visitant. There was no use to alarm the household, which did not seem to have been disturbed. The trespassers were far away by this time, and the attempt would hardly be repeated that night. He made his way quietly back to the corral, let loose his horse, and regained the *casa* unobserved. He unlocked the arched door in the wall, reëntered the darkened passage, stopped a moment to open the door of the boudoir, glance at the closely fastened casement, and extinguish the still burning candle, and, relocking the door securely, made his way to his own room.

But he could not sleep. The whole incident, over so quickly, had nevertheless impressed him deeply, and yet like a dream. The strange yell of the vacquero still rang in his ears, but with an unearthly and superstitious significance that was even more dreamlike in its meaning. He awakened from a fitful slumber to find the light of morning in the room, and Incarnacion standing by his bedside.

The yellow face of the steward was greenish with terror, and his lips were dry.

"Get up, Señor Clarencio; get up at

once, my master. Strange things have happened. Mother of God protect us!"

Clarence rolled to his feet, with the events
of the past night struggling back upon his
consciousness.

"What mean you, Nascio?" he said,
grasping the man's arm, which was still
mechanically making the sign of the cross,
as he muttered incoherently. "Speak, I
command you!"

"It is José, the little vacquero, who is
even now at the *padre's* house, raving as a
lunatic, stricken as a madman with terror!
He has seen him, — the dead alive! Save
us!"

"Are you mad yourself, Nascio?" said
Clarence. "Whom has he seen?"

"Whom? God help us! the old *padron* —
Señor Peyton himself! He rushed towards
him here, in the *patio*, last night — out of
the air, the sky, the ground, he knew not,
— his own self, wrapped in his old storm
cloak and hat, and riding his own horse, —
erect, terrible, and menacing, with an awful
hand upholding a rope — so! He saw him
with these eyes, as I see you. What *he* said
to him, God knows! The priest, perhaps,
for he has made confession!"

In a flash of intelligence Clarence comprehended all. He rose grimly and began to dress himself.

"Not a word of this to the women, — to any one, Nascio, dost thou understand?" he said curtly. "It may be that José has been partaking too freely of aguardiente, — it is possible. I will see the priest myself. But what possesses thee? Collect thyself, good Nascio."

But the man was still trembling.

"It is not all, — Mother of God! it is not all, master!" he stammered, dropping to his knees and still crossing himself. "This morning, beside the corral, they find the horse of Pedro Valdez splashed and spattered on saddle and bridle, and in the stirrup, — dost thou hear? the *stirrup,* — hanging, the torn-off boot of Valdez! Ah, God! The same as *his!* Now do you understand? It is *his* vengeance. No! Jesu forgive me! it is the vengeance of God!"

Clarence was staggered.

"And you have not found Valdez? You have looked for him?" he said, hurriedly throwing on his clothes.

"Everywhere, — all over the plain. The whole rancho has been out since sunrise, —

here and there and everywhere. And there is nothing! Of course not. What would you?" He pointed solemnly to the ground.

"Nonsense!" said Clarence, buttoning his coat and seizing his hat. "Follow me."

He ran down the passage, followed by Incarnacion, through the excited, gesticulating crowd of servants in the *patio*, and out of the back gate. He turned first along the wall of the *casa* towards the barred window of the boudoir. Then a cry came from Incarnacion.

They ran quickly forward. Hanging from the grating of the window, like a mass of limp and saturated clothes, was the body of Pedro Valdez, with one unbooted foot dangling within an inch of the ground. His head was passed inside the grating and fixed as at that moment when the first spring of the frightened horse had broken his neck between the bars as in a garrote, and the second plunge of the terrified animal had carried off his boot in the caught stirrup when it escaped.

CHAPTER XI.

THE winter rains were over and gone,
and the whole long line of Californian coast
was dashed with color. There were miles
of yellow and red poppies, leagues of lupines that painted the gently rounded hills
with soft primary hues, and long continuous
slopes, like low mountain systems, of daisies
and dandelions. At Sacramento it was
already summer; the yellow river was flashing and intolerable; the tule and marsh
grasses were lush and long; the bloom of
cottonwood and sycamore whitened the outskirts of the city, and as Cyrus Hopkins
and his daughter Phœbe looked from the
veranda of the Placer Hotel, accustomed as
they were to the cool trade winds of the
coast valleys, they felt homesick from the
memory of eastern heats.

Later, when they were surveying the long
dinner tables at the table d'hôte with something of the uncomfortable and shamefaced
loneliness of the provincial, Phœbe uttered

a slight cry and clutched her father's arm.
Mr. Hopkins stayed the play of his squared
elbows and glanced inquiringly at his daughter's face. There was a pretty animation in
it, as she pointed to a figure that had just
entered. It was that of a young man attired in the extravagance rather than the
taste of the prevailing fashion, which did
not, however, in the least conceal a decided
rusticity of limb and movement. A long
mustache, which looked unkempt, even in
its pomatumed stiffness, and lank, dark
hair that had bent but never curled under
the barber's iron, made him notable even in
that heterogeneous assembly.

"That 's he," whispered Phœbe.

"Who?" said her father.

Alas for the inconsistencies of love! The
blush came with the name and not the vision.

"Mr. Hooker," she stammered.

It was, indeed, Jim Hooker. But the
rôle of his exaggeration was no longer the
same; the remorseful gloom in which he had
been habitually steeped had changed into a
fatigued, yet haughty, fastidiousness more
in keeping with his fashionable garments.
He was more peaceful, yet not entirely

placable, and, as he sat down at a side table and pulled down his striped cuffs with his clasped fingers, he cast a glance of critical disapproval on the general company. Nevertheless, he seemed to be furtively watchful of his effect upon them, and as one or two whispered and looked towards him, his consciousness became darkly manifest.

All of which might have intimidated the gentle Phœbe, but did not discompose her father. He rose, and crossing over to Hooker's table, clapped him heartily on the back.

"How do, Hooker? I did n't recognize you in them fine clothes, but Phœbe guessed as how it was you."

Flushed, disconcerted, irritated, but always in wholesome awe of Mr. Hopkins, Jim returned his greeting awkwardly and half hysterically. How he would have received the more timid Phœbe is another question. But Mr. Hopkins, without apparently noticing these symptoms, went on: —

"We 're only just down, Phœbe and me, and as I guess we 'll want to talk over old times, we 'll come alongside o' your. Hold on, and I 'll fetch her."

The interval gave the unhappy Jim a

chance to recover himself, to regain his vanished cuffs, display his heavy watch-chain,
curl his mustache, and otherwise reassume
his air of blasé fastidiousness. But the
transfer made, Phœbe, after shaking hands,
became speechless under these perfections.
Not so her father.

"If there 's anything in looks, you seem
to be prospering," he said grimly; "unless
you 're in the tailorin' line, and you 're
only showin' off stock. What mout ye be
doing?"

"Ye ain't bin long in Sacramento, I
reckon?" suggested Jim, with patronizing
pity.

"No, we only came this morning," returned Hopkins.

"And you ain't bin to the theatre?" continued Jim.

"No."

"Nor moved much in — in — gin'ral
fash'nable sassiety?"

"Not yet," interposed Phœbe, with an
air of faint apology.

"Nor seen any of them large posters on
the fences, of 'The Prairie Flower; or, Red-
handed Dick,' — three - act play with five
tableaux, — just the biggest sensation out,

— runnin' for forty nights, — money turned away every night, — standin' room only?" continued Jim, with prolonged toleration.

"No."

"Well, *I* play Red - handed Dick. I thought you might have seen it and recognized me. All those people over there," darkly indicating the long table, "know me. A fellow can't stand it, you know, being stared at by such a vulgar, low-bred lot. It's gettin' too fresh here. I'll have to give the landlord notice and cut the whole hotel. They don't seem to have ever seen a gentleman and a professional before."

"Then you're a play-actor now?" said the farmer, in a tone which did not, however, exhibit the exact degree of admiration which shone in Phœbe's eyes.

"For the present," said Jim, with lofty indifference. "You see I was in — in partnership with McClosky, the manager, and I didn't like the style of the chump that was doin' Red-handed Dick, so I offered to take his place one night to show him how. And by Jinks! the audience, after that night, wouldn't let anybody else play it, — wouldn't stand even the biggest, highest-priced stars in it! I reckon," he added gloomily, "I'll have to run the darned thing in all the big towns in Californy, — if I don't have to go East with it after all, just for the business. But it's an awful grind on a man, — leaves him no time, along of the invitations he gets, and what with being run after in the streets and stared at in the hotels he don't get no privacy. There's men, and women, too, over at that table, that just lie in wait for me here till I come, and don't lift their eyes off me. I wonder they don't bring their opery-glasses with them."

Concerned, sympathizing, and indignant, poor Phœbe turned her brown head and honest eyes in that direction. But because they were honest, they could not help observing that the other table did not seem to be paying the slightest attention to the distinguished impersonator of Red-handed Dick. Perhaps he had been overheard.

"Then that was the reason ye did n't come back to your location. I always guessed it was because you 'd got wind of the smash-up down there, afore we did," said Hopkins grimly.

"What smash-up?" asked Jim, with slightly resentful quickness.

"Why, the smash - up of the Sisters'
title, — did n't you hear that?"

There was a slight movement of relief
and a return of gloomy hauteur in Jim's
manner.

"No, we don't know much of what goes
on in the cow counties, up here."

"Ye mout, considerin' it concerns some
o' your friends," returned Hopkins dryly.
"For the Sisters' title went smash as soon
as it was known that Pedro Valdez — the
man as started it — had his neck broken
outside the walls o' Robles Rancho; and
they do say as this yer Brant, *your* friend,
had suthin' to do with the breaking of it,
though it was laid to the ghost of old Peyton.   Anyhow, there was such a big skeer
that one of the Greaser gang, who thought
he 'd seen the ghost, being a Papist, to save
his everlasting soul went to the priest and
confessed.   But the priest would n't give
him absolution until he 'd blown the hull
thing, and made it public.   And then it
turned out that all the dockyments for the
title, and even the custom - house paper,
were *forged* by Pedro Valdez, and put on
the market by his confederates.   And that 's
just where *your* friend, Clarence Brant,

comes in, for *he* had bought up the whole title from them fellers. Now, either, as some say, he was in the fraud from the beginnin', and never paid anything, or else he was an all-fired fool, and had parted with his money like one. Some allow that the reason was that he was awfully sweet on Mrs. Peyton's adopted daughter, and ez the parents did n't approve of him, he did *this* so as to get a holt over them by the property. But he's a ruined man, anyway, now; for they say he's such a darned fool that he's goin' to pay for all the improvements that the folks who bought under him put into the land, and that 'll take his last cent. I thought I'd tell you that, for I suppose *you* 've lost a heap in your improvements, and will put in your claim?"

"I reckon I put nearly as much into it as Clar Brant did," said Jim gloomily, "but I ain't goin' to take a cent from him, or go back on him now."

The rascal could not resist this last mendacious opportunity, although he was perfectly sincere in his renunciation, touched in his sympathy, and there was even a film of moisture in his shifting eyes.

Phœbe was thrilled with the generosity of

this noble being, who could be unselfish even in his superior condition. She added softly: —

"And they say that the girl did not care for him at all, but was actually going to run off with Pedro, when he stopped her and sent for Mrs. Peyton."

To her surprise, Jim's face flushed violently.

"It 's all a dod-blasted lie," he said, in a thick stage whisper. "It 's only the hogwash them Greasers and Pike County galoots ladle out to each other around the stove in a county grocery. But," recalling himself loftily, and with a tolerant wave of his bediamonded hand, "wot kin you expect from one of them cow counties? They ain't satisfied till they drive every gentleman out of the darned gopher-holes they call their 'kentry.'"

In her admiration of what she believed to be a loyal outburst for his friend, Phœbe overlooked the implied sneer at her provincial home. But her father went on with a perfunctory, exasperating, dusty aridity: —

"That mebbee ez mebbee, Mr. Hooker, but the story down in our precinct goes that she gave Mrs. Peyton the slip, — chucked up her situation as adopted darter, and went off with a queer sort of a cirkiss woman, — one of her own *kin*, and I reckon one of her own *kind*."

To this Mr. Hooker offered no further reply than a withering rebuke of the waiter, a genteel abstraction, and a lofty change of subject. He pressed upon them two tickets for the performance, of which he seemed to have a number neatly clasped in an india-rubber band, and advised them to come early. They would see him after the performance and sup together. He must leave them now, as he had to be punctually at the theatre, and if he lingered he should be pestered by interviewers. He withdrew under a dazzling display of cuff and white handkerchief, and with that inward swing of the arm and slight bowiness of the leg generally recognized in his profession as the lounging exit of high comedy.

The mingling of awe and an uneasy sense of changed relations which that meeting with Jim had brought to Phœbe was not lessened when she entered the theatre with her father that evening, and even Mr. Hopkins seemed to share her feelings. The theatre was large, and brilliant in decora-

tion, the seats were well filled with the same
heterogeneous mingling she had seen in the
dining-room at the Placer Hotel, but in the
parquet were some fashionable costumes and
cultivated faces. Mr. Hopkins was not
altogether so sure that Jim had been "only
gassing." But the gorgeous drop curtain,
representing an allegory of Californian
prosperity and abundance, presently up-
rolled upon a scene of Western life almost
as striking in its glaring unreality. From
a rose-clad English cottage in a subtropical
landscape skipped "Rosalie, the Prairie
Flower." The briefest of skirts, the most
unsullied of stockings, the tiniest of slip-
pers, and the few diamonds that glittered
on her fair neck and fingers, revealed at
once the simple and unpretending daughter
of the American backwoodsman. A tumult
of delighted greeting broke from the audience. The bright color came to the pink,
girlish cheeks, gratified vanity danced in
her violet eyes, and as she piquantly bowed
her acknowledgments, this great breath of
praise seemed to transfigure and possess her.
A very young actor who represented the
giddy world in a straw hat and with an effeminate manner was alternately petted and

girded at by her during the opening exposition of the plot, until the statement that a "dark destiny" obliged her to follow her uncle in an emigrant train across the plains closed the act, apparently extinguished him, and left *her* the central figure. So far, she evidently was the favorite. A singular aversion to her crept into the heart of Phœbe.

But the second act brought an Indian attack upon the emigrant train, and here "Rosalie" displayed the archest heroism and the pinkest and most distracting self-possession, in marked contrast to the giddy worldling who, having accompanied her apparently for comic purposes best known to himself, cowered abjectly under wagons, and was pulled ignominiously out of straw, until Red Dick swept out of the wings with a chosen band and a burst of revolvers and turned the tide of victory. Attired as a picturesque combination of the Neapolitan smuggler, river-bar miner, and Mexican vacquero, Jim Hooker instantly began to justify the plaudits that greeted him and the most sanguinary hopes of the audience. A gloomy but fascinating cloud of gunpowder and dark intrigue from that moment hung about the stage.

Yet in this sombre obscuration Rosalie
had passed a happy six months, coming out
with her character and stockings equally
unchanged and unblemished, to be rewarded
with the hand of Red Dick and the discovery of her father, the governor of New
Mexico, as a white-haired, but objectionable
vacquero, at the fall of the curtain.

Through this exciting performance Phœbe
sat with a vague and increasing sense of
loneliness and distrust.   She did not know
that Hooker had added to his ordinary in-
ventive exaggeration the form of dramatic
composition.   But she had early detected
the singular fact that such shadowy outlines
of plot as the piece possessed were evidently
based on his previous narrative of his *own*
experiences, and the saving of Susy Peyton
— by himself!   There was the episode of
their being lost on the plains, as he had already related it to her, with the addition of
a few years to Susy's age and some vivid
picturesqueness to himself as Red Dick.
She was not, of course, aware that the part
of the giddy worldling was Jim's own conception of the character of Clarence.   But
what, even to her provincial taste, seemed
the extravagance of the piece, she felt, in

some way, reflected upon the truthfulness
of the story she had heard. It seemed to
be a parody on himself, and in the laughter
which some of the most thrilling points produced in certain of the audience, she heard
an echo of her own doubts. But even this
she could have borne if Jim's confidence
had not been given to the general public; it
was no longer *hers* alone, she shared it with
them. And this strange, bold girl, who
acted with him, — the "Blanche Belville"
of the bills, — how often he must have told
her the story, and yet how badly she had
learned it! It was not her own idea of it,
nor of *him*. In the last extravagant scene
she turned her weary and half-shamed eyes
from the stage and looked around the theatre. Among a group of loungers by the
wall a face that seemed familiar was turned
towards her own with a look of kindly and
sympathetic recognition. It was the face of
Clarence Brant. When the curtain fell,
and she and her father rose to go, he was
at their side. He seemed older and more
superior looking than she had ever thought
him before, and there was a gentle yet sad
wisdom in his eyes and voice that comforted
her even while it made her feel like, crying.

"You are satisfied that no harm has come to our friend," he said pleasantly. "Of course you recognized him?"

"Oh, yes; we met him to-day," said Phœbe. Her provincial pride impelled her to keep up a show of security and indifference. "We are going to supper with him."

Clarence slightly lifted his brows.

"You are more fortunate than I am," he said smilingly. "I only arrived here at seven, and I must leave at midnight."

Phœbe hesitated a moment, then said with affected carelessness: —

"What do you think of the young girl who plays with him? Do you know her? Who is she?"

He looked at her quickly, and then said, with some surprise: —

"Did he not tell you?"

"No."

"She *was* the adopted daughter of Mrs. Peyton, — Miss Susan Silsbee," he said gravely.

"Then she *did* run away from home as they said," said Phœbe impulsively.

"Not *exactly* as they said," said Clarence gently. "She elected to make her home with her aunt, Mrs. McClosky, who is the

wife of the manager of this theatre, and she
adopted the profession a month ago. As
it now appears that there was some infor-
mality in the old articles of guardianship,
Mrs. Peyton would have been powerless to
prevent her from doing either, even if she
had wished to."

The infelicity of questioning Clarence
regarding Susy suddenly flashed upon the
forgetful Phœbe, and she colored. Yet, although sad, he did not look like a rejected
lover.

"Of course, if she is here with her own
relatives, that makes all the difference," she
said gently. "It is protection."

"Certainly," said Clarence.

"And," continued Phœbe hesitatingly,
"she is playing with — with — an old friend
— Mr. Hooker!"

"That is quite proper, too, considering
their relations," said Clarence tolerantly.

"I — don't — understand," stammered
Phœbe.

The slightly cynical smile on Clarence's
face changed as he looked into Phœbe's
eyes.

"I 've just heard that they are married,"
he returned gently.

CHAPTER XII.

NOWHERE had the long season of flowers brought such glory as to the broad plains and slopes of Robles Rancho. By some fortuitous chance of soil, or flood, or drifting pollen, the three terraces had each taken a distinct and separate blossom and tint of color. The straggling line of corral, the crumbling wall of the old garden, the outlying chapel, and even the brown walls of the *casa* itself, were half sunken in the tall racemes of crowding lupines, until from the distance they seemed to be slowly settling in the profundity of a dark-blue sea. The second terrace was a league-long flow of gray and gold daisies, in which the cattle dazedly wandered mid-leg deep. A perpetual sunshine of yellow dandelions lay upon the third. The gentle slope to the dark-green *cañada* was a broad cataract of crimson poppies. Everywhere where water had stood, great patches of color had taken its place. It seemed as if the rains had ceased

only that the broken heavens might drop
flowers.

Never before had its beauty — a beauty
that seemed built upon a cruel, youthful,
obliterating forgetfulness of the past —
struck Clarence as keenly as when he had
made up his mind that he must leave the
place forever. For the tale of his mis-
chance and ill-fortune, as told by Hopkins,
was unfortunately true. When he discovered that in his desire to save Peyton's
house by the purchase of the Sisters' title
he himself had been the victim of a gigantic
fraud, he accepted the loss of the greater
part of his fortune with resignation, and
was even satisfied by the thought that he
had at least effected the possession of the
property for Mrs. Peyton. But when he
found that those of his tenants who had
bought under him had acquired only a du-
bious possession of their lands and no title,
he had unhesitatingly reimbursed them for
their improvements with the last of his capital. Only the lawless Gilroy had good-
humoredly declined. The quiet acceptance
of the others did not, unfortunately, pre-
clude their settled belief that Clarence had
participated in the fraud, and that even now

his restitution was making a dangerous pre-
cedent, subversive of the best interests of
the State, and discouraging to immigration.
Some doubted his sanity.   Only one, struck
with the sincerity of his motive, hesitated
to take his money, with a look of commis-
eration on his face.

"Are you not satisfied?" asked Clarence,
smiling.

"Yes, but" —

"But what?"

"Nothin'.   Only I was thinkin' that a
man like you must feel awful lonesome in
Calforny!"

Lonely he was, indeed; but his loneliness
was not the loss of fortune nor what it
might bring.   Perhaps he had never fully
realized his wealth; it had been an accident
rather than a custom of his life, and when
it had failed in the only test he had made
of its power, it is to be feared that he only
sentimentally regretted it.   It was too early
yet for him to comprehend the veiled bless-
ings of the catastrophe in its merciful dis-
ruption of habits and ways of life; his loneliness was still the hopeless solitude left by
vanished ideals and overthrown idols.   He
was satisfied that he had never cared for

Susy, but he still cared for the belief that he had.

After the discovery of Pedro's body that fatal morning, a brief but emphatic interview between himself and Mrs. McClosky had followed. He had insisted upon her immediately accompanying Susy and himself to Mrs. Peyton in San Francisco. Horror-stricken and terrified at the catastrophe, and frightened by the strange looks of the excited servants, they did not dare to disobey him. He had left them with Mrs. Peyton in the briefest preliminary interview, during which he spoke only of the catastrophe, shielding the woman from the presumption of having provoked it, and urging only the importance of settling the question of guardianship at once. It was odd that Mrs. Peyton had been less disturbed than he imagined she would be at even his charitable version of Susy's unfaithfulness to her; it even seemed to him that she had already suspected it. But as he was about to withdraw to leave her to meet them alone, she had stopped him suddenly.

"What would you advise me to do?"

It was his first interview with her since

the revelation of his own feelings. He looked into the pleading, troubled eyes of the woman he now knew he had loved, and stammered: —

"You alone can judge. Only you must remember that one cannot force an affection any more than one can prevent it."

He felt himself blushing, and, conscious of the construction of his words, he even fancied that she was displeased.

"Then you have no preference?" she said, a little impatiently.

"None."

She made a slight gesture with her handsome shoulders, but she only said, "I should have liked to have pleased you in this," and turned coldly away. He had left without knowing the result of the interview; but a few days later he received a letter from her stating that she had allowed Susy to return to her aunt, and that she had resigned all claims to her guardianship.

"It seemed to be a foregone conclusion," she wrote; "and although I cannot think such a change will be for her permanent welfare, it is her present *wish*, and who knows, indeed, if the change will be permanent? I have not allowed the legal question to interfere with my judgment, although her friends must know that she forfeits any claim upon the estate by her action; but at the same time, in the event of her suitable marriage, I should try to carry out what I believe would have been Mr. Peyton's wishes."

There were a few lines of postscript: "It seems to me that the change would leave you more free to consult your own wishes in regard to continuing your friendship with Susy, and upon such a footing as may please you. I judge from Mrs. McClosky's conversation that she believed you thought you were only doing your duty in reporting to me, and that the circumstances had not altered the good terms in which you all three formerly stood."

Clarence had dropped the letter with a burning indignation that seemed to sting his eyes until a scalding moisture hid the words before him. What might not Susy have said? What exaggeration of his affection was she not capable of suggesting? He recalled Mrs. McClosky, and remembered her easy acceptance of him as Susy's lover. What had they told Mrs. Peyton? What must be her opinion of his deceit towards

herself? It was hard enough to bear this
before he knew he loved her. It was intolerable now! And this is what she meant
when she suggested that he should renew
his old terms with Susy; it was for *him*
that this ill-disguised, scornful generosity
in regard to Susy's pecuniary expectations
was intended. What should he do? He
would write to her, and indignantly deny
any clandestine affection for Susy. But
could he do that, in honor, in truthfulness?
Would it not be better to write and confess
all? Yes, — *everything.*

Fortunately for his still boyish impulsiveness, it was at this time that the discovery
of his own financial ruin came to him. The
inquest on the body of Pedro Valdez and
the confession of his confidant had revealed
the facts of the fraudulent title and forged
testamentary documents. Although it was
correctly believed that Pedro had met his
death in an escapade of gallantry or intrigue,
the coroner's jury had returned a verdict of
"accidental death," and the lesser scandal
was lost in the wider, far-spreading disclos-
ure of fraud. When he had resolved to
assume all the liabilities of his purchase, he
was obliged to write to Mrs. Peyton and

confess his ruin. But he was glad to remind her that it did not alter *her* status or security; he had only given her the possession, and she would revert to her original and now uncontested title. But as there was now no reason for his continuing the stewardship, and as he must adopt some profession and seek his fortune elsewhere, he begged her to relieve him of his duty. Albeit written with a throbbing heart and suffused eyes, it was a plain, business-like, and practical letter. Her reply was equally cool and matter of fact. She was sorry to hear of his losses, although she could not agree with him that they could logically sever his present connection with the rancho, or that, placed upon another and distinctly business footing, the occupation would not be as remunerative to him as any other. But, of course, if he had a preference for some more independent position, that was another question, although he would forgive her for using the privilege of her years to remind him that his financial and business success had not yet justified his independence. She would also advise him not to decide hastily, or, at least, to wait until she had again thoroughly gone over her husband's papers with her lawyer, in reference to the old purchase of the Sisters' title, and the conditions under which it was bought. She knew that Mr. Brant would not refuse this as a matter of business, nor would that friendship, which she valued so highly, allow him to imperil the possession of the rancho by leaving it at such a moment. As soon as she had finished the examination of the papers, she would write again. Her letter seemed to leave him no hope, if, indeed, he had ever indulged in any. It was the practical kindliness of a woman of business, nothing more. As to the examination of her husband's papers, that was a natural precaution. He alone knew that they would give no record of a transaction which had never occurred. He briefly replied that his intention to seek another situation was unchanged, but that he would cheerfully await the arrival of his successor. Two weeks passed. Then Mr. Sanderson, Mrs. Peyton's lawyer, arrived, bringing an apologetic note from Mrs. Peyton. She was so sorry her business was still delayed, but as she had felt that she had no right to detain him entirely at Robles, she had sent to Mr. Sanderson to *temporarily* relieve him, that he

might be free to look around him or visit
San Francisco in reference to his own business, only extracting a promise from him
that he would return to Robles to meet her
at the end of the week, before settling upon
anything.

The bitter smile with which Clarence had
read thus far suddenly changed. Some
mysterious touch of unbusiness-like but womanly hesitation, that he had never noticed
in her previous letters, gave him a faint
sense of pleasure, as if her note had been
perfumed. He had availed himself of the
offer. It was on this visit to Sacramento
that he had accidentally discovered the marriage of Susy and Hooker.

"It's a great deal better business for her
to have a husband in the 'profesh' if she's
agoin' to stick to it," said his informant,
Mrs. McClosky, "and she's nothing if she
ain't business and profesh, Mr. Brant. I
never see a girl that was born for the stage
— yes, you might say jess cut out o' the
boards of the stage — as that girl Susy is!
And that's jest what's the matter; and *you*
know it, and *I* know it, and there you are!"

It was with these experiences that Clarence was to-day reëntering the wooded and

rocky gateway of the rancho from the high
road of the *cañada ;* but as he cantered up
the first slope, through the drift of scarlet
poppies that almost obliterated the track,
and the blue and yellow blooms of the terraces again broke upon his view, he thought
only of Mrs. Peyton's pleasure in this
changed aspect of her old home. She had
told him of it once before, and of her delight in it; and he had once thought how
happy he should be to see it with her.

The servant who took his horse told him
that the señora had arrived that morning
from Santa Inez, bringing with her the two
Señoritas Hernandez from the rancho of
Los Canejos, and that other guests were
expected. And there was the Señor Sanderson and his Reverence Padre Esteban.
Truly an affair of hospitality, the first since
the *padron* died. Whatever dream Clarence might have had of opportunities for
confidential interview was rudely dispelled.
Yet Mrs. Peyton had left orders to be informed at once of Don Clarencio's arrival.

As he crossed the *patio* and stepped upon
the corridor he fancied he already detected
in the internal arrangements the subtle influence of Mrs. Peyton's taste and the inde-

finable domination of the mistress. For an
instant he thought of anticipating the servant and seeking her in the boudoir, but
some instinct withheld him, and he turned
into the study which he had used as an office.
It was empty; a few embers glimmered on
the hearth. At the same moment there was
a light step behind him, and Mrs. Peyton
entered and closed the door behind her.
She was very beautiful. Although paler
and thinner, there was an odd sort of animation about her, so unlike her usual repose
that it seemed almost feverish.

"I thought we could talk together a few
moments before the guests arrive. The
house will be presently so full, and my
duties as hostess commence."

"I was — about to seek you — in — in the
boudoir," hesitated Clarence.

She gave an impatient shiver.

"Good heavens, not there! I shall never
go there again. I should fancy every time
I looked out of the window that I saw the
head of that man between the bars. No!
I am only thankful that I wasn't here at
the time, and that I can keep my remembrance of the dear old place unchanged."
She checked herself a little abruptly, and

then added somewhat irrelevantly but cheerfully, "Well, you have been away? What
have you done?"

"Nothing," said Clarence.

"Then you have kept your promise," she
said, with the same nervous hilarity.

"I have returned here without making
any other engagement," he said gravely;
"but I have not altered my determination."

She shrugged her shoulders again, or, as
it seemed, the skin of her tightly fitting
black dress above them, with the sensitive
shiver of a highly groomed horse, and moved
to the hearth as if for warmth; put her slim,
slippered foot upon the low fender, drawing,
with a quick hand, the whole width of her
skirt behind her until it clingingly accented
the long, graceful curve from her hip to
her feet. All this was so unlike her usual
fastidiousness and repose that he was struck
by it. With her eyes on the glowing embers of the hearth, and tentatively advan-
cing her toe to its warmth and drawing it
away, she said: —

"Of course, you must please yourself. I
am afraid I have no right except that of
habit and custom to keep you here; and you
know," she added, with an only half-with-

held bitterness, "that they are not always very effective with young people who prefer to have the ordering of their own lives. But I have something still to tell you before you finally decide. I have, as you know, been looking over my — over Mr. Peyton's papers very carefully. Well, as a result, I find, Mr. Brant, that there is no record whatever of his wonderfully providential purchase of the Sisters' title from you; that he never entered into any written agreement with you, and never paid you a cent; and that, furthermore, his papers show me that he never even contemplated it; nor, indeed, even knew of *your* owning the title when he died. Yes, Mr. Brant, it was all to *your* foresight and prudence, and *your* generosity alone, that we owe our present possession of the rancho. When you helped us into that awful window, it was *your* house we were entering; and if it had been *you*, and not those wretches, who had chosen to shut the doors on us after the funeral, we could never have entered here again. Don't deny it, Mr. Brant. I have suspected it a long time, and when you spoke of changing *your* position, I determined to find out if it was n't *I* who had to leave the house rather

than you. One moment, please. And I
did find out, and it *was* I. Don't speak,
please, yet. And now," she said, with a
quick return to her previous nervous hilarity, "knowing this, as you did, and knowing, too, that I would know it when I examined the papers, — don't speak, I'm not
through yet, — don't you think that it was
just a *little* cruel for you to try to hurry me,
and make me come here instead of your
coming to *me* in San Francisco, when I gave
you leave for that purpose?"

"But, Mrs. Peyton," gasped Clarence.

"Please don't interrupt me," said the
lady, with a touch of her old imperiousness,
"for in a moment I must join my guests.
When I found you would n't tell me, and
left it to me to find out, I could only go
away as I did, and really leave you to control what I believed was your own property.
And I thought, too, that I understood your
motives, and, to be frank with you, *that*
worried me; for I believed I knew the dis-
position and feelings of a certain person
better than yourself."

"One moment," broke out Clarence, "you
must hear me, now. Foolish and misguided
as that purchase may have been, I swear to

you I had only one motive in making it, —
to save the homestead for you and your husband, who had been my first and earliest
benefactors. What the result of it was,
you, as a business woman, know; your
friends know; your lawyer will tell you the
same. You owe me nothing. I have given
you nothing but the repossession of this
property, which any other man could have
done, and perhaps less stupidly than I did.
I would not have forced you to come here
to hear this if I had dreamed of your suspicions, or even if I had simply understood
that you would see me in San Francisco as
I passed through."

"Passed through? Where were you going?" she said quickly.

"To Sacramento."

The abrupt change in her manner startled
him to a recollection of Susy, and he
blushed. She bit her lips, and moved
towards the window.

"Then you saw her?" she said, turning
suddenly towards him. The inquiry of her
beautiful eyes was more imperative than her
speech.

Clarence recognized quickly what he
thought was his cruel blunder in touching

the half-healed wound of separation. But
he had gone too far to be other than perfectly truthful now.

"Yes; I saw her on the stage," he said,
with a return of his boyish earnestness;
"and I learned something which I wanted
you to first hear from me. She is *married,*
— and to Mr. Hooker, who is in the same
theatrical company with her. But I want
you to think, as I honestly do, that it is the
best for her. She has married in her profession, which is a great protection and a
help to her success, and she has married a
man who can look lightly upon certain qual-
ities in her that others might not be so
lenient to. His worst faults are on the surface, and will wear away in contact with the
world, and he looks up to her as his superior. I gathered this from her friend, for
I did not speak with her myself; I did not
go there to see her. But as I expected to
be leaving you soon, I thought it only right
that as I was the humble means of first
bringing her into your life, I should bring
you this last news, which I suppose takes
her out of it forever. Only I want you to
believe that *you* have nothing to regret, and
that *she* is neither lost nor unhappy."

The expression of suspicious inquiry on her face when he began changed gradually to perplexity as he continued, and then relaxed into a faint, peculiar smile. But there was not the slightest trace of that pain, wounded pride, indignation, or anger, that he had expected to see upon it.

"That means, I suppose, Mr. Brant, that *you* no longer care for her?"

The smile had passed, yet she spoke now with a half-real, half-affected archness that was also unlike her.

"It means," said Clarence with a white face, but a steady voice, "that I care for her now as much as I ever cared for her, no matter to what folly it once might have led me. But it means, also, that there was no time when I was not able to tell it to *you* as frankly as I do now" —

"One moment, please," she interrupted, and turned quickly towards the door. She opened it and looked out. "I thought they were calling me, — and — I — I — *must* go now, Mr. Brant. And without finishing my business either, or saying half I had intended to say. But wait" — she put her hand to her head in a pretty perplexity, "it's a moonlight night, and I'll propose after dinner a stroll in the gardens, and you can manage to walk a little with me." She stopped again, returned, said, "It was very kind of you to think of me at Sacramento," held out her hand, allowed it to remain for an instant, cool but acquiescent, in his warmer grasp, and with the same odd youthfulness of movement and gesture slipped out of the door.

An hour later she was at the head of her dinner table, serene, beautiful, and calm, in her elegant mourning, provokingly inaccessible in the sweet deliberation of her widowed years; Padre Esteban was at her side with a local magnate, who had known Peyton and his wife, while Donna Rosita and a pair of liquid-tongued, childlike señoritas were near Clarence and Sanderson. To the priest Mrs. Peyton spoke admiringly of the changes in the rancho and the restoration of the Mission Chapel, and together they had commended Clarence from the level of their superior passionless reserve and years. Clarence felt hopelessly young and hopelessly lonely; the naïve prattle of the young girls beside him appeared infantine. In his abstraction, he heard Mrs. Peyton allude to the beauty of the night, and propose that after coffee and chocolate the ladies should put on their wraps and go with her to the old garden. Clarence raised his eyes; she was not looking at him, but there was a slight consciousness in her face that was not there before, and the faintest color in her cheek, still lingering, no doubt, from the excitement of conversation.

It was a cool, tranquil, dewless night when they at last straggled out, mere black and white patches in the colorless moonlight. The brilliancy of the flower-hued landscape was subdued under its passive, pale austerity; even the gray and gold of the second terrace seemed dulled and confused. At any other time Clarence might have lingered over this strange effect, but his eyes followed only a tall figure, in a long striped burnous, that moved gracefully beside the *soutaned* priest. As he approached, it turned towards him.

"Ah! here you are. I just told Father Esteban that you talked of leaving to-morrow, and that he would have to excuse me a few moments while you showed me what you had done to the old garden."

She moved beside him, and, with a hesitation that was not unlike a more youthful

timidity, slipped her hand through his arm.
It was for the first time, and, without thinking, he pressed it impulsively to his side.
I have already intimated that Clarence's
reserve was at times qualified by singular
directness.

A few steps carried them out of hearing;
a few more, and they seemed alone in the
world. The long adobe wall glanced away
emptily beside them, and was lost; the black
shadows of the knotted pear-trees were beneath their feet. They began to walk with
the slight affectation of treading the shadows as if they were patterns on a carpet.
Clarence was voiceless, and yet he seemed
to be moving beside a spirit that must be
first addressed.

But it was flesh and blood nevertheless.

"I interrupted you in something you were
saying when I left the office," she said'
quietly.

"I was speaking of Susy," returned Clarence eagerly; "and" —

"Then you need n't go on," interrupted
Mrs. Peyton quickly. "I understand you,
and believe you. I would rather talk of
something else. We have not yet arranged
how I can make restitution to you for the

capital you sank in saving this place. You
will be reasonable, Mr. Brant, and not leave
me with the shame and pain of knowing
that you ruined yourself for the sake of your
old friends. For it is no more a sentimental idea of mine to feel in this way than it is
a fair and sensible one for you to imply that
a mere quibble of construction absolves me
from responsibility. Mr. Sanderson himself admits that the repossession you gave
us is a fair and legal basis for any arrangement of sharing or division of the property
with you, that might enable you to remain
here and continue the work you have so well
begun. Have you no suggestion, or must
it come from *me*, Mr. Brant? "

"Neither. Let us not talk of that now."

She did not seem to notice the boyish
doggedness of his speech, except so far as it
might have increased her inconsequent and
nervously pitched levity.

"Then suppose we speak of the Misses
Hernandez, with whom you scarcely exchanged a word at dinner, and whom I
invited for you and your fluent Spanish.
They are charming girls, even if they are a
little stupid. But what can I do? If I am
to live here, I must have a few young people

around me, if only to make the place cheerful for others. Do you know I have taken
a great fancy to Miss Rogers, and have
asked her to visit me. I think she is a good
friend of yours, although perhaps she is a
little shy. What's the matter? You have
nothing against her, have you?"

Clarence had stopped short. They had
reached the end of the pear-tree shadows.
A few steps more would bring them to the
fallen south wall of the garden and the open
moonlight beyond, but to the right an olive
alley of deeper shadow diverged.

"No," he said, with slow deliberation;
"I have to thank Mary Rogers for having
discovered something in me that I have
been blindly, foolishly, and hopelessly struggling with."

"And, pray, what was that?" said Mrs.
Peyton sharply.

"That I love you!"

Mrs. Peyton was fairly startled. The
embarrassment of any truth is apt to be in
its eternal abruptness, which no devious-
ness of tact or circumlocution of diplomacy
has ever yet surmounted. Whatever had
been in her heart, or mind, she was unprepared for this directness. The bolt had

dropped from the sky; they were alone; there was nothing between the stars and the earth but herself and this man and this truth; it could not be overlooked, surmounted, or escaped from. A step or two more would take her out of the garden into the moonlight, but always into this awful frankness of blunt and outspoken nature. She hesitated, and turned the corner into the olive shadows. It was, perhaps, more dangerous; but less shameless, and less like truckling. And the appallingly direct Clarence instantly followed.

"I know you will despise me, hate me; and, perhaps, worst of all, disbelieve me; but I swear to you, now, that I have always loved you, — yes, *always!* When first I came here, it was not to see my old playmate, but *you*, for I had kept the memory of you as I first saw you when a boy, and you have always been my ideal. I have thought of, dreamed of, worshiped, and lived for no other woman. Even when I found Susy again, grown up here at your side; even when I thought that I might, with your consent, marry her, it was that I might be with *you* always; that I might be a part of *your* home, your family, and have a place with her in *your* heart; for it was you I loved, and *you* only. Don't laugh at me, Mrs. Peyton, it is the truth, the whole truth, I am telling you. God help me!"

If she only *could* have laughed, — harshly, ironically, or even mercifully and kindly! But it would not come. And she burst out: —

"I am not laughing. Good heavens, don't you see? It is *me* you are making ridiculous."

" *You* ridiculous?" he said in a momentarily choked, half-stupefied voice. "You — a beautiful woman, my superior in everything, the mistress of these lands where I am only steward — made ridiculous, not by my presumption, but by my confession? Was the saint you just now admired in Father Esteban's chapel ridiculous because of the *peon* clowns who were kneeling before it?"

"Hush! This is wicked! Stop!"

She felt she was now on firm ground, and made the most of it in voice and manner. She must draw the line somewhere, and she would draw it beween passion and impiety.

"Not until I have told you all, and I

must before I leave you. I loved you when
I came here, — even when your husband
was alive. Don't be angry, Mrs. Peyton;
he would not, and need not, have been angry; he would have pitied the foolish boy,
who, in the very innocence and ignorance
of his passion, might have revealed it to him
as he did to everybody but *one*. And yet,
I sometimes think you might have guessed
it, had you thought of me at all. It must
have been on my lips that day I sat with
you in the boudoir. I know that I was
filled with it; with it and with you; with
your presence, with your beauty, your grace
of heart and mind, — yes, Mrs. Peyton,
even with your own unrequited love for
Susy. Only, then, I knew not what it
was."

"But I think *I* can tell you what it was
then, and now," said Mrs. Peyton, recover-
ing her nervous little laugh, though it died
a moment after on her lips. "I remember
it very well. You told me then that *I reminded you of your mother.* Well, I am
not old enough to be your mother, Mr.
Brant, but I am old enough to have been,
and might have been, the mother of your
wife. That was what you meant then; that

is what you mean now. I was wrong to ac-
cuse you of trying to make me ridiculous.
I ask your pardon. Let us leave it as it
was that day in the boudoir, as it is *now.*
Let me still remind you of your mother, —
I know she must have been a good woman to
have had so good a son, — and when you
have found some sweet young girl to make
you happy, come to me for a mother's blessing, and we will laugh at the recollection
and misunderstanding of this evening."

Her voice did not, however, exhibit that
exquisite maternal tenderness which the
beatific vision ought to have called up, and
the persistent voice of Clarence could not
be evaded in the shadow.

"I said you reminded me of my mother,"
he went on at her side, "because I knew
her and lost her only as a child. She never
was anything to me but a memory, and yet
an ideal of all that was sweet and lovable in
woman. Perhaps it was a dream of what
she might have been when she was as young
in years as you. If it pleases you still to
misunderstand me, it may please you also
to know that there is a reminder of her even
in this. I have no remembrance of a word
of affection from her, nor a caress; I have

been as hopeless in my love for her who was
my mother, as of the woman I would make
my wife."

"But you have seen no one, you know no
one, you are young, you scarcely know your
own self! You will forget this, you will
forget *me!* And if — if — I should — listen
to you, what would the world say, what
would *you* yourself say a few years hence?
Oh, be reasonable. Think of it, — it would
be so wild, — so mad! so — so — utterly
ridiculous!"

In proof of its ludicrous quality, two tears
escaped her eyes in the darkness. But
Clarence caught the white flash of her withdrawn handkerchief in the shadow, and captured her returning hand. It was trembling, but did not struggle, and presently
hushed itself to rest in his.

"I'm not only a fool but a brute," he
said in a lower voice. "Forgive me. I
have given you pain, — you, for whom I
would have died."

They had both stopped. He was still
holding her sleeping hand. His arm had
stolen around the burnous so softly that it
followed the curves of her figure as lightly
as a fold of the garment, and was presum-

ably unfelt. Grief has its privileges, and suffering exonerates a questionable situation. In another moment her fair head *might* have dropped upon his shoulder. But an approaching voice uprose in the adjoining broad *allée.* It might have been the world speaking through the voice of the lawyer Sanderson.

"Yes, he is a good fellow, and an intelligent fellow, too, but a perfect child in his experience of mankind."

They both started, but Mrs. Peyton's hand suddenly woke up and grasped his firmly. Then she said in a higher, but perfectly level tone: —

"Yes, I think with you we had better look at it again in the sunlight to-morrow. But here come our friends; they have probably been waiting for us to join them and go in."

.   .   .   .

The wholesome freshness of early morning was in the room when Clarence awoke, cleared and strengthened. His resolution had been made. He would leave the rancho that morning, to enter the world again and seek his fortune elsewhere. This was only right to *her,* whose future it should never be

said he had imperiled by his folly and inexperience; and if, in a year or two of struggle
he could prove his right to address her again,
he would return. He had not spoken to her
since they had parted in the garden, with
the grim truths of the lawyer ringing in his
ears, but he had written a few lines of fare-
well, to be given to her after he had left.
He was calm in his resolution, albeit a little
pale and hollow-eyed for it.

He crept downstairs in the gray twilight
of the scarce-awakened house, and made his
way to the stables. Saddling his horse, and
mounting, he paced forth into the crisp
morning air. The sun, just risen, was everywhere bringing out the fresh color of the
flower-strewn terraces, as the last night's
shadows, which had hidden them, were
slowly beaten back. He cast a last look at
the brown adobe quadrangle of the quiet
house, just touched with the bronzing of the
sun, and then turned his face towards the
highway. As he passed the angle of the
old garden he hesitated, but, strong in his
resolution, he put the recollection of last
night behind him, and rode by without raising his eyes.

"Clarence!"

It was *her* voice. He wheeled his horse.
She was standing behind the *grille* in the
old wall as he had seen her standing on the
day he had ridden to his rendezvous with
Susy. A Spanish *manta* was thrown over
her head and shoulders, as if she had dressed
hastily, and had run out to intercept him
while he was still in the stable. Her beautiful face was pale in its black-hooded recess, and there were faint circles around her
lovely eyes.

"You were going without saying 'goodby'!" she said softly.

She passed her slim white hand between
the grating. Clarence leaped to the ground,
caught it, and pressed it to his lips. But
he did not let it go.

"No! no!" she said, struggling to withdraw it. "It is better as it is — as — as
you have decided it to be. Only I could
not let you go thus, — without a word.
There now, — go, Clarence, go. Please!
Don't you see I am behind these bars?
Think of them as the years that separate us,
my poor, dear, foolish boy. Think of them
as standing between us, growing closer,
heavier, and more cruel and hopeless as the
years go on."

Ah, well! they had been good bars a hundred and fifty years ago, when it was thought as necessary to repress the innocence that was behind them as the wickedness that was without. They had done duty in the convent at Santa Inez, and the monastery of Santa Barbara, and had been brought hither in Governor Micheltorrenas' time to keep the daughters of Robles from the insidious contact of the outer world, when they took the air in their cloistered pleasance. Guitars had tinkled against them in vain, and they had withstood the stress and storm of love tokens. But, like many other things which have had their day and time, they had retained their semblance of power, even while rattling loosely in their sockets, only because no one had ever thought of putting them to the test, and, in the strong hand of Clarence, assisted, perhaps, by the leaning figure of Mrs. Peyton, I grieve to say that the whole *grille* suddenly collapsed, became a frame of tinkling iron, and then clanked, bar by bar, into the road. Mrs. Peyton uttered a little cry and drew back, and Clarence, leaping the ruins, caught her in his arms.

For a moment only, for she quickly withdrew from them, and although the morning sunlight was quite rosy on her cheeks, she said gravely, pointing to the dismantled opening : —

"I suppose you *must* stay now, for you never could leave me here alone and defenseless."

He stayed. And with this fulfillment of his youthful dreams the romance of his young manhood seemed to be completed, and so closed the second volume of this trilogy. But what effect that fulfillment of youth had upon his maturer years, or the fortunes of those who were nearly concerned in it, may be told in a later and final chronicle.

Bret Harte.

Works. *Riverside Edition*, rearranged. With Portrait and Introduction. In 6 vols. crown 8vo, each $2.00. The set, $12.00; half calf, $18.00; half calf, gilt top, $19.50.

1. Poetical Works, Two Men of Sandy Bar, Introduction, and Portrait. 2. The Luck of Roaring Camp, and other Stories, a portion of the Tales of the Argonauts, etc. 3. Tales of the Argonauts and Eastern Sketches. 4. Gabriel Conroy. 5. Stories, and Condensed Novels. 6. Frontier Stories.

The Luck of Roaring Camp, and Other Sketches. 16mo, $1.25.

The Luck of Roaring Camp, and other Stories. In Riverside Aldine Series. 16mo, $1.00.

These volumes are not identical in contents.

Mrs. Skaggs's Husbands, etc. 16mo, $1.25.
Tales of the Argonauts, etc. 16mo, $1.25.
Thankful Blossom. 18mo, $1.00.
Two Men of Sandy Bar. A Play. 18mo, $1.00.
The Story of a Mine. 18mo, $1.00.
Drift from Two Shores. 18mo, $1.00.
The Twins of Table Mountain. 18mo, $1.00.
Flip, and Found at Blazing Star. 18mo, $1.00.
In the Carquinez Woods. 18mo, $1.00.
On the Frontier. Stories. 18mo, $1.00.
By Shore and Sedge. 18mo, $1.00.
Maruja. 18mo, $1.00.
Snow-Bound at Eagle's. 18mo, $1.00.
A Millionaire of Rough-and-Ready, and Devil's Ford. 18mo, $1.00.
A Phyllis of the Sierras, and Drift from Redwood Camp. 18mo, $1.00.
The Argonauts of North Liberty. 18mo, $1.00.
A Waif of the Plains. 18mo, $1.00.
Novels and Tales. 15 vols. 18mo, $15.00.
Cressy. 16mo, $1.25.
The Crusade of the Excelsior. Illustrated. 16mo, $1.25 ; paper, 50 cents.

See next page.

HOUGHTON, MIFFLIN & CO., Publishers.

Bret Harte (*continued*).

The Heritage of Dedlow Marsh, etc. 16mo, $1.25.

A Ward of the Golden Gate. 16mo, $1.25; paper, 50 cents.

A Sappho of Green Springs, and other Stories. 16mo, $1.25.

A First Family of Tasajara. 16mo, $1.25.

Colonel Starbottle's Client, and Some Other People. 16mo, $1.25.

Susy. A Story of the Plains. 16mo.

Wilhelm Hauff.

Arabian Days' Entertainments. Translated by Herbert Pelham Curtis. Illustrated. 12mo, $1.50.

Octave Thanet.

Knitters in the Sun. 16mo, $1.25.

Otto the Knight, and other Stories. 16mo, $1.25.

Edmund Quincy.

The Haunted Adjutant, and other Stories. 12mo, $1.50.

Wensley, and other Stories. 12mo, $1.50.

J. P. Quincy.

The Peckster Professorship. 16mo, $1.25.

Gen. Lew Wallace.

The Fair God; or, The Last of the 'Tzins. A Tale of the Conquest of Mexico. 12mo, $1.50.

Henry Watterson (editor).

Oddities in Southern Life and Character. With Illustrations by Sheppard and Church. 16mo, $1.50.

Fergus Hume.

Aladdin in London. A Romance. 16mo, $1.25.

HOUGHTON, MIFFLIN & CO., Publishers.

Charles Egbert Craddock [Mary N. Murfree].

In the Tennessee Mountains. Short Stories. 16mo, $1.25.

Down the Ravine. For Young People. Illustrated. 16mo, $1.00.

The Prophet of the Great Smoky Mountains. 16mo, $1.25.

In the Clouds. 16mo, $1.25.

The Story of Keedon Bluffs. 16mo, $1.00.

The Despot of Broomsedge Cove. 16mo, $1.25.

Where the Battle was Fought. 16mo, $1.25.

Joel Chandler Harris.

Mingo, and other Sketches in Black and White. 16mo, $1.25 ; paper, 50 cents.

Nights with Uncle Remus. Illustrated. 12mo, $1.50 ; paper, 50 cents.

Baalam and his Master, and other Stories. 16mo, $1.25.

Uncle Remus and His Friends. Old Plantation Stories, Songs, and Ballads. With Sketches of Negro Character. With 12 Illustrations by Frost. 12mo, $1.50.

Joseph Kirkland.

Zury : The Meanest Man in Spring County. A Novel of Western Life. With Frontispiece. 12mo, $1.50; paper, 50 cents.

The McVeys. 16mo, $1.25.

Charles and Mary Lamb.

Tales from Shakespeare. 16mo, $1.00.

Handy-Volume Edition. 24mo, gilt top, $1.00.

The Same. Illustrated. 16mo, $1.00.

Luigi Monti.

Leone. 16mo, $1.00 ; paper, 50 cents.

HOUGHTON, MIFFLIN & CO., Publishers.

James Fenimore Cooper.

Works. New *Household Edition*. With Introductions to many of the volumes by SUSAN FENIMORE COOPER, and Illustrations. In 32 volumes. Each, 16mo, $1.00; the set, $32.00; half calf, $64.00.

Precaution.	Wept of Wish-ton-Wish.
The Spy.	The Water-Witch.
The Pioneers.	The Bravo.
The Pathfinder.	Red Rover.
Mercedes of Castile.	Homeward Bound.
The Deerslayer.	Home as Found.
The Red Skins.	The Heidenmauer.
The Chainbearer.	The Headsman.
Satanstoe.	The Two Admirals.
The Crater.	The Pilot.
Afloat and Ashore.	Lionel Lincoln.
The Prairie.	Last of the Mohicans.
Wing and Wing.	Jack Tier.
Wyandotté.	The Sea Lions.
The Monikins.	Oak Openings.
Miles Wallingford.	Ways of the Hour.

New Edition. With Portrait, Illustrations, and Introductions. In 32 vols. 16mo, gilt top, $32.00. (*Sold only in sets.*)

Fireside Edition. With Portrait, Introductions, and 43 Illustrations. In 16 vols. 12mo, $20.00; half calf, $40.00. (*Sold only in sets.*)

Sea Tales. First Series. New *Household Edition*. With Introductions by Susan Fenimore Cooper. Illustrated. In 5 vols., the set, 16mo, $5.00; half calf, $10.00.

Sea Tales. Second Series. New *Household Edition*. With Introductions by Susan Fenimore Cooper. Illustrated. In 5 vols., the set, 16mo, $5.00; half calf, $10.00.

Leather Stocking Tales. New *Household Edition*. With Portrait, Introductions, and Illustrations. In 5 vols., the set, 16mo, $5.00; half calf, $10.00.

Cooper Stories. Narratives of Adventure selected from Cooper's Works. Illustrated. Stories of the Prairie. Stories of the Woods. Stories of the Sea. 3 vols. 16mo, $1.00 each; the set, $3.00.

The Spy. 16mo, paper, 50 cents.

HOUGHTON, MIFFLIN & CO., Publishers.